CANOEiNG

The Essential Skills and Safety

ALSO AVAILABLE

Outdoor Parents, Outdoor Kids
$19.95

Sea Kayaking Rough Waters
$19.95

Winter Backpacking
$19.95

Ice Fishing: The Ultimate Guide
$24.95

Kayak Fishing: The Ultimate Guide 2nd Edition
$24.95

Kayak Bass Fishing
$24.95

Recreational Kayaking The Ultimate Guide
$19.95

Whitewater Kayaking The Ultimate Guide—2nd Edition
$26.95

Kayaking for Fitness
$19.95

Camp Cooking in the Wild
$19.95

Rolling a Kayak
$16.95

Canoe Camping
$16.95

Touring & Sea Kayaking The Essential Skills and Safety
$19.95

Torrent
$29.95

The Playboater's Handbook II
$22.95

Kayak Fishing: Game On 2 DVD
$24.95

Filleting Fish—Freshwater DVD
$12.95

Running The Essential Guide DVD
$19.95

Knots to Know DVD
$14.96

Whitewater Kayaking—DVD Box Set
$49.95

Kayak Fishing: Game On DVD
$24.95

Kayak Fishing The Ultimate Guide DVD
$19.95

Canoeing with Andrew Westwood DVD
$19.95

Rolling a Kayak—Whitewater DVD
$26.95

Rolling a Kayak—Sea Kayak DVD
$26.95

Recreational Kayaking The Essential Skills and Safety DVD
$19.95

Recreational Kayaking for Women DVD
$24.95

b.EAST DVD
$19.95

Sea Kayaking: The Ultimate Guide DVD
$29.95

Whitewater Kayaking with Ken Whiting DVD
$29.95

Playboating with Ken Whiting DVD
$29.95

The Paddling Chef, Second Edition
$16.95

CANOEING
The Essential Skills and Safety

Andrew Westwood
Photography by Paul Villecourt

THE **HELICONIA** PRESS

an Imprint of Fox Chapel Publishing
www.FoxChapelPublishing.com

Written by: Andrew Westwood
Photography by: Paul Villecourt
Design and Layout: Robyn Hader
Edited by: Rebecca Sandiford

ISBN 978-1-896980-69-0

Library of Congress Cataloging-in-Publication Data

Westwood, Andrew.

Canoeing / by Andrew Westwood ; photos by Paul Villecourt ; [edited by Rebecca Sandiford].

   p. cm.

Originally published : Ontario, Canada : Heliconia Press, c2007.

Includes index.

ISBN 978-1-896980-69-0 (alk. paper)

1. Canoes and canoeing. 2. Canoes and canoeing--Training. 3. Canoes and canoeing--Safety measures. I. Sandiford, Rebecca II. Title.

GV783W44 2012

797.122--dc23

                          2011051812

To learn more about the other great books from Fox Chapel Publishing, or to find a retailer near you,
call toll-free 800-457-9112 or visit us at www.FoxChapelPublishing.com.

Note to Authors: We are always looking for talented authors to write new books. Please send a brief letter describing your idea to Acquisition Editor, 1970 Broad Street, East Petersburg, PA 17520.

Printed in China
First printing

TABLE OF CONTENTS

INTRODUCTION TO CANOEING

Whether relaxing silently amongst reeds watching wildlife, or pulling firmly on a paddle to cross a remote lake on a wilderness journey, the canoe is the ultimate watercraft for adventure travel in North America. Vast networks of waterways and portage trails provide endless possibilities for exploring, whether for an afternoon or a multi-day trip. The canoeing skills needed to discover this wilderness beauty can be learned easily by anyone. This book will provide the essentials of flat water canoeing and the background information you'll need to join in the adventure.

Rich with lakes and rivers, North America has long been home to the canoe. No other craft so effectively opened up the New World to European commerce and trade. Today, the popularity of canoes is witnessed by all who travel our highways during the summer. You'll see canoe-topped cars heading to watery destinations all across this land. There are virtually no limits to where canoes can go. They are light, paddled easily by one or two people, and fun to take exploring.

The elegance and simplicity of the classic canoe shape gives it an incredible versatility. Today's canoes are used for such diverse paddling disciplines as canoe dance, marathon racing and steep whitewater descents on mountainous creeks. This book however, focuses on the flat water canoeing and the skills needed to enjoy lakes and slow moving rivers, either as a tandem pair, or as a solo paddler. Be prepared though—canoeing is addictive, and you may find yourself impassioned to regularly explore the great outdoors in this magical craft.

Whether you are new to canoeing or brushing up on your paddling skills, The Essentials of Flat water Canoeing will provide current information to guide you on your future paddling adventures. Imagine silently dipping your paddle as you cross a mirror-smooth lake shrouded in morning mist—with each stroke of the paddle, the canoe moves you forward through nature, toward adventure, and onward to self-discovery. So grab a paddle, let's go canoeing!

ABOUT THE AUTHOR

Andrew Westwood is a wilderness canoe adventurer, whitewater paddler and open canoe slalom competitor living in Ottawa, Ontario, Canada. He has instructed canoeing extensively in both Canada and the United States for over 15 years. Passionate about canoeing, he shares his insights by authoring instructional articles and has worked in both canoe design and marketing for prominent paddlesport companies. As a successful open canoe athlete, he has garnered many first place finishes in international slalom events. At home in the wilderness, he has guided on the Nahanni River, the North Shore of Lake Superior and explored areas of Ellesmere Island in Canada's far north.

To my wife Carole, who also shares a passion for paddling, thank you for all your help and support in writing this book and for being the perfect partner, both in the canoe and at home.

To those reading this book, I hope you are as fortunate as I to enjoy many outdoor adventures in a canoe. The rewards of paddling are measured by good memories, great friendships and the satisfaction of exploring our waterways in style—from the seat of a canoe.

EQUIPMENT

1

THE CANOE

THE PADDLE

PERSONAL GEAR

THE CANOE

Beautiful in both form and function, canoes display graceful lines and a balanced shape that can effectively transport paddler and gear to almost any watery destination.

Though sharing a common appearance, canoes come in many shapes and sizes. The character and performance of each boat will be greatly influenced by construction material, length, width and depth. Some canoes are built to satisfy a particular type of use, from wilderness pickup truck to whitewater sports car. Some canoes are paddled solo, some tandem, and some are designed for either. Voyager canoes can accommodate a dozen or more paddlers. The common element throughout is that the canoe is powered by at least one sitting or kneeling paddler holding a single-bladed paddle. In this book we're going to focus on flat water canoes.

A two-person (tandem) flat water canoe is typically 15 to 18 feet long. Solo canoes average 14 to 16 feet. Widths range from 30 to 37 inches with depths close to 15 inches. For lake water paddling, many paddlers look to tandem canoes that are reasonably light and around 16 feet in length. A 15- or 16-foot tandem canoe can also serve double duty as a respectable solo canoe too.

Canoes are built from many durable materials that balance the need for structural strength without sacrificing weight efficiency. Popular today are composite boats made of Kevlar, polyester cloth, fiberglass or a mix of these products to produce canoes that are both lightweight and strong. For the truly weight-conscious, carbon fiber canoes represent the lightest boats available. For unsurpassed strength, plastic canoes are the most durable and low-maintenance, but be prepared to live with some extra weight.

In the light-weight category, Kevlar and carbon fiber composite canoes may weigh as little as 40 pounds for a 16-foot canoe. Desirable for their ease in portaging, these canoes are also the most fragile. In the mid-weight range, 60-pound fiberglass canoes are common and combine good strength and easy lift weight for a typical 16-foot canoe. Heavier still are tough, low maintenance Royalex plastic canoes. For general use, lighter versions of Royalex canoes may weigh as little as 65 pounds, or as much as 75 pounds for an expedition-grade canoe capable of withstanding hard use on extended wilderness trips. Cedar/canvas canoes represent a more traditional look and feel, and range in weight from about 55 to 75 pounds. Although needing periodic maintenance, these canoes have the smoothest feeling on the water and are a joy to paddle.

If you plan on doing much portaging, the lightness of a Kevlar canoe will be much appreciated.

CANOE DESIGN AND SELECTION

The canoe has been around for hundreds of years, and its time-tested form has changed little from the crafts first paddled by Native North Americans. However, contemporary materials and modern hull shapes continue to evolve and new models of canoes are being added to an already long list of well-established traditional canoe models. Every canoe shape represents a blend of different performance characteristics. Canoe designs balance the traits of stability, speed, straight-line tracking, maneuverability, weight, and carrying capacity.

Selecting your own canoe depends on finding one that feels right. Each hull shape has its own individual feel. If you are choosing a canoe for the fist time, start with a general purpose design that balances all the performance traits and take the demo model for a test paddle. Then, if you wish to get more of one particular feature, try another canoe noted for this feature and feel the difference in performance. The staff at any good store that sells canoes should be able to help you zero in on one you'll like.

Be aware that an exceptional characteristic usually comes at the expense of some other feature. Look for these compromises: faster hulls tend to be less stable, canoes large enough for long canoe trips tend to be less maneuverable, and light-weight canoes tend to be more fragile. The good news is that with so many canoe models available the canoe of your dreams is just a few test paddles away!

ROCKER

Most canoes are gently arched along the bottom of the hull when viewed from bow to stern. The ends, or stems, usually rest higher in the water due to this curvature of the hull bottom. This is called the canoe's rocker. More rocker refers to a canoe with more upturned ends, and less rocker indicates a canoe which is flatter on the bottom. More rocker helps a canoe turn more quickly and may even contribute to a drier ride in big waves. A flatter rocker is characteristic of faster canoes that go more easily in a straight line known as tracking, and these are terrific for cruising.

LENGTH

Canoe length affects the cargo capacity of the hull and ultimately determines how fast a canoe can travel. Remember, speed is not everything. Maneuverability, ease of portaging and the potential for solo paddling are also important considerations when choosing the length of a canoe. Longer canoes are faster and carry more weight than shorter ones, but are more difficult to portage, put on your vehicle and paddle in windy conditions. If you are looking for maximum hull efficiency or a boat for expeditions, 17- to 18-foot models are the speedy choices.

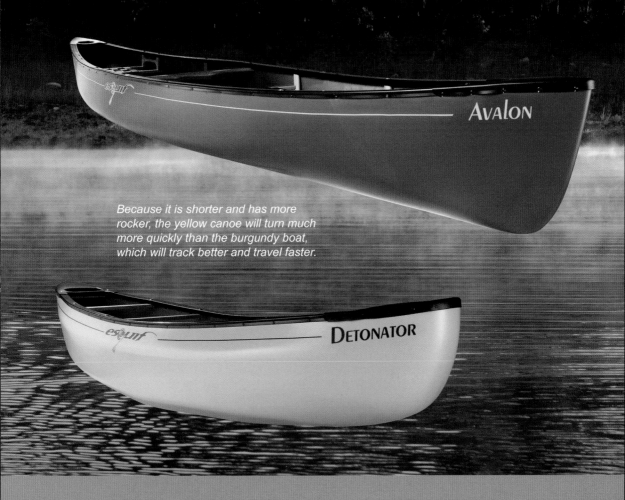

Because it is shorter and has more rocker, the yellow canoe will turn much more quickly than the burgundy boat, which will track better and travel faster.

Shorter canoes are generally more versatile because they can be paddled tandem or solo. They are very maneuverable, are much lighter and suffer less in windy conditions. Typically around 15 feet in length, these models carry less gear and are more susceptible to taking in a bit of water when paddling tandem in rough and wavy conditions.

A good length for general all-purpose paddling is the 16-foot canoe. It achieves a balance in meeting the demands for speed, stability, carrying capacity, maneuverability and can be easily paddled tandem or solo.

WIDTH

Canoe widths vary on average between 30 to 37 inches. Wide canoes are more stable and slower than narrow canoes. Canoes wide in the beam can carry a family of two adults and two small children in relative security. Narrow canoes are efficient and more easily paddled solo. Good recreational canoes usually measures 35 to 36 inches between the gunwales at the widest point.

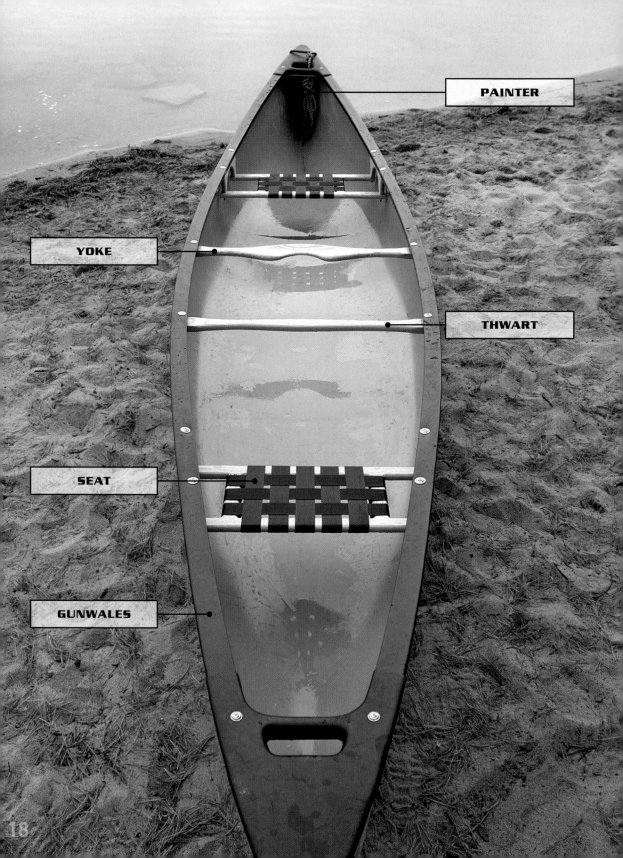

PAINTER

YOKE

THWART

SEAT

GUNWALES

18

YOKES, THWARTS AND SEATS

The yoke is the piece across the middle of the boat that is used when the canoe is carried by one person. If you ever intend to carry your canoe this way, treat yourself to a carved wooden yoke, which will rest more comfortably on your shoulders when the boat is being carried. Sometimes a yoke will just be a metal bar, which can be very uncomfortable for carrying on your shoulders. You can always attach foam to a yoke to make it more comfortable.

The thwarts are the other pieces of metal or wood that cross the canoe width-wise and are also part of the canoe's structural integrity. Occasionally there is one in the bow end of the boat and one in the stern end. In some cases canoes are equipped with a kneeling thwart located between the center thwart and the stern seat. The kneeling thwart is used for solo paddling as it allows you to sit near the middle of the canoe where your strokes are more effective for boat control.

Traditional seats are frequently made of wood and have a woven deck for comfort and ventilation. A handy option in tandem canoes is the sliding bow seat. These seats are mounted on rails that allow you to slide the seat forward and backward to better trim (balance) the canoe. For example, if the bow person is considerably lighter than the stern partner, then the seat can be slid forward to level the trim and keep the canoe resting almost flat in the water. This will make the canoe easier to paddle and control.

GUNWALES

Gunwales (pronounced "gunnels") go around the top rim of the hull and are made of metal or wood. To some extent, gunwales help the canoe hold its form and are part of the boat's structural integrity, plus they provide a smooth edge around the boat. Wood gunwales require more care and maintenance, but they feel great and will generally be easier on your paddle, as it will come in contact with the gunwales for some strokes.

SIDES

An important design feature of many canoes is the side shape. Flared hulls have a side profile that gradually widens from the waterline upward to the gunwales. Flare helps to keep the canoe dry in wavy conditions and enhances stability. Canoes that narrow above the waterline, toward the gunwale, have a shape called tumblehome. Tumblehome can make canoes less stable if tipped too far to the side, but the benefit of tumblehome is that the curved side of the canoe allows your paddle to reach the water more comfortably. Tumblehome also favors solo canoeing especially if the canoe is paddled in a traditional style where it is heeled (leaned) over on its side.

CHINE

The chine is the area where the sides of the canoe meet the bottom of the hull. The sharpness or softness of this curve will affect how secure the canoe feels when it is tilted to the side. Soft, rounded chines deliver greater canoe stability, while boats with sharper chines may feel more tippy. Some paddlers choose sharp chines to help the canoe carve turns in a tighter arc, which helps make a canoe very maneuverable.

HULL SHAPES

Canoes are often classified as having a particular hull shape. Each shape has an inherent performance advantage and disadvantage. To reduce the negative effect of any hull shape, canoe designers often mix different hull shapes into one canoe model. For example, the bow may have one shape, the middle another hull shape and a third for the stern. This is a real bonus for paddlers as they can select from so many canoe models exhibiting a terrific range of paddling characteristics.

Arched hull

An arched hull describes the round curve from side to side under the canoe. A more rounded hull will give you more speed, but may feel unstable to beginners. Softer, less rounded hulls are still quick, but offer greater stability.

Flat hull

Flat hulls give canoes astounding stability but slow them down considerably. This will make the canoe seem heavy and sluggish to paddle. A flat hull may be helpful if you plan to do most of your paddling with children or a high-energy dog.

V hull

The V-shaped hull is a compromise used to provide both speed and stability. The V hull also helps make it easier to paddle a canoe in a straight line, or track—an attractive feature for beginners. The down side to this hull type is that it tends to be more cumbersome to turn around sharp bends.

SIDES
Tumblehome vs. Flare

Tumblehome sides curve inward toward the gunwale and allow more comfortable strokes, while flared sides are angled outward and help keep the canoe dry in waves.

HULLS
Flat | Arched | V

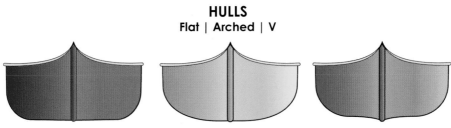

*Flat hulls provide superior stability, arched hulls are good for speed,
and V-hulls provide exceptional tracking.*

THE PADDLE

Canoeing bathes the senses with a spectacular array of sights, sounds and smells. Most impressive though, is the sense of touch—feeling the buoyancy of the canoe as it floats on the water and the tactile sensation of the water through the paddle in your hands. A paddle has to feel right to you. Balance, weight and texture are just some of the things to consider when choosing a paddle.

With few exceptions, canoe paddles used for lake paddling are made of wood. Wood has the most flexibility to cushion the force of strokes on your body's joints. The strength and light weight of wooden paddles lessens fatigue and keeps the paddle feeling "alive" even after a full day of canoeing. Wood is also easily fashioned into the most efficient shapes to satisfy different tastes in paddling style and other personal preferences.

Paddles can be prepared from a solid piece of wood, or can be laminated from a variety of wood types to enhance strength and weight characteristics. Aesthetics are much appreciated by most canoeists, so paddle makers often go to great lengths to highlight wood grain with creative designs and finishes. A paddle can last a lifetime and is often a work of art, so feel free to choose with an eye for both beauty and practicality.

Paddle length is directly proportional to your height. Although paddles are referenced by their overall length, the true measure of interest is the overall shaft length—blade lengths and shape vary considerably. To protect your shoulder joints and to help maintain your balance in the canoe, you must select a paddle that has the correct shaft length for your size. Paddle lengths for adults range from about 50 to 62 inches. Retail stores often stock paddles with length increases of 2 inch increments. As you might guess, the taller and longer-limbed you are, the longer your paddle should be. In the 'Holding a Paddle' segment of this book, we look at a quick technique for establishing your hand position, which also lets you test whether or not a paddle is the right length for you.

Blade size and shape will have a significant impact on the performance and feel of the paddle. Blade shapes range from rectangular to oblong. Slender Voyager style paddles have blades with smaller surface areas and are more comfortable for distance paddling as they hold less water on the blade face. This gives the paddle a lighter, livelier feel. Wider blades, such as the Beaver and Otter Tail, tend to have a slightly larger surface area and therefore catch more water on each stroke. Although heavier, the performance provided by a larger, squarer blade is needed when negotiating swift currents or running rapids. All paddle blades should have a fine tapered edge to permit a clean (splash-free) entry into the water

A Voyager paddle, a Beaver Tail paddle, and a Bent Shaft paddle each have pros and cons.

PERSONAL GEAR

Being well-equipped for flat water canoeing will make for a more comfortable trip and one that is safer too! Dressing for the conditions and being prepared for changes in the weather makes good sense. Canoeing requires that everyone have a life jacket, or personal floatation device (PFD). For safety, consider brightly colored clothing to make sure you are clearly visible to other boating traffic. Another advantage to bright clothing is that if you paddle where you'll encounter mosquitoes and black flies, bright and neutral colors attract fewer insects than darker colors.

PFD

PFDs are the most important safety device to canoeists. They should be approved by the Coast Guard and selected to match the required buoyancy for the user's weight. Try on different PFDs to find a comfortable fit. It should be adjustable to allow a snug fit while worn over different thicknesses of clothing. If a PFD is fitted properly, you should not be able to pull it up over your head once it is cinched tight. A quick and easy fit test is to hook your thumbs under the shoulder straps and pull upward. It should stay in place and not rise up to your chin. Although many colors are available, consider brightly colored PFDs or those with reflective tape, because they are more easily seen in the event of an emergency. It is also essential to outfit your PFD with a whistle for communication.

A PFDs buoyancy is provided by closed cell foam, which is also an effective insulator. If paddling in cooler temperatures, choose a PFD shaped more like a jacket so it can offer an additional layer of insulation. Vest style PFDs provide the greatest freedom of movement for performing canoe strokes. Vests are the obvious choice for hot climates to reduce the risk of over heating. Be wary of PFDs equipped with multiple pockets – fully loaded, the pockets can impede your movements and weigh you down if you capsize.

Paddling-specific PFDs are ideal because they are comfortable to wear and offer complete freedom of movement.

In warm conditions, your biggest concern will often be to protect yourself from the sun.

DRESSING FOR WARM CONDITIONS

Staying cool in hot summer conditions may be as simple as going for a swim in the lake. Ignoring the early signs of overheating may lead to heat stroke, dehydration, or simply sun burn. Dressing for warm conditions will add to your overall enjoyment of canoeing and reduce the risk of overheating. A hat, sunglasses and sunscreen are essential items for sun protection. Light-colored, loose-fitting clothing allow freedom of movement, sun protection and are breathable. If it is slightly cooler out, synthetics like polypropylene or fleece are excellent choices because they dry quickly if splashed, and continue to insulate you when they're wet, unlike cotton, which actually draws heat away from your body when it's wet.

Even warm summer days can turn uncomfortably cold when sudden winds or thunderstorms occur. Having a protective shell handy for sudden changes in the weather is a good idea. Waterproof/breathable fabrics are a great choice for wind and rain protection. Wearing a shell that is both waterproof and breathable keeps rain from penetrating the jacket while allowing perspiration to evaporate through the jacket from the inside. The performance goal for these jackets is to keep you dry, both from the outside and from the inside. Paddlers often choose garments made of "Gore-Tex" or a similar waterproof/breathable material.

Traditional rainwear, cut long in the body and equipped with a hood, works well for most outdoor activities, and may suffice for canoeing. The downside to wearing rain jackets is that the excess fabric can hamper your swimming efforts if you capsize. Superior performance can be achieved by wearing a long-sleeved or short-sleeved paddling jacket. Designed as active wear, paddling jackets offer the greatest freedom of movement and can be used as part of a layering strategy with other synthetic clothing. Adding to their utility, paddling jackets often have neck and wrist closures that seal out water. Paddling jackets are available in waterproof/breathable materials or can be purchased less expensively if made with a polyurethane coating. A word of caution: if you perspire heavily, condensation inside a polyurethane-coated jacket may make you wet and cold.

Canoeing can be demanding on footwear. Expect your feet to get wet. Quality sandals and water shoes such as those made by Teva or Keen allow the freedom to step out of a canoe and into the water without the feeling of being bogged down by heavy wet footwear afterward. The downside to many sandals is that they provide poor foot protection when walking along rocky shores and root-riddled trails. Consider a water-friendly day hiker for foot protection if portaging is part of your paddling route.

DRESSING FOR COLD CONDITIONS

Comfort in cold conditions depends on layering multiple pieces of clothing to manage the moisture produced as an inevitable by-product of being active. Keeping dry is almost as important as keeping warm when preventing the threat of hypothermia. By wearing a couple of layers of clothing you can regulate your comfort by adding or removing layers in response to feeling hot or cold.

There are three basic layers; a wicking layer, an insulation layer and an outer protective shell. For the wicking layer choose silk, wool or synthetics such as polypropylene and capilene. These layers offer warmth and moisture transfer from your skin to the outer insulation layers. Fleece and wool are favored choices for the insulation layer. Synthetics have a slight advantage over wool as they are more hydrophobic (don't absorb much water) and dry very quickly. Outer shell layers must be breathable to allow body moisture to escape to the environment, away from the body, and windproof to protect against wind-chill.

Clothing made of cotton is not recommended for cold water paddling. Cotton is very slow to dry, absorbs perspiration and draws heat away from your body. In colder conditions, wearing cotton next to the skin can quickly lead to hypothermia.

A paddle jackets is a great piece of gear to bring along. Made from waterproof and breathable fabric, a paddle jacket fits comfortably over insulating layers and under your PFD to protect you from wind and water.

SAFETY GEAR & ACCESSORIES

Canoeing is a very safe form of travel. Even non-swimmers who wear a properly-fitted PFD will be able to cope well if the canoe capsizes. Exposure to the elements tends to be the most significant risk that paddlers have to prepare themselves for. Being able to respond quickly to a situation will increase the chances of a good outcome

The following list of equipment is aimed at canoeists who want to plan a day outing. Each day out on the water may bring different circumstances that will require unique preparations. Your choice of equipment may depend on how remote the area is in which you are paddling, the variability of the weather conditions, and water temperature. A comprehensive list of gear necessary for longer distance canoe trips is covered in another book in the Essential Guide Series, entitled Canoe Camping.

EMERGENCY KIT

Even day outings can be packed with surprises. For example, unforeseen changes in weather may require protective clothing or even a temporary shelter. In some cases, conditions might necessitate spending a night ashore. Consider the implications of stubbornly paddling into a storm, or perhaps past dusk, just because you do not have adequate gear for a night out. Paddling beyond our comfort zone, or worse, in unsafe conditions, may lead to disaster. Effective planning will make an unwelcome situation safer and much more bearable.

Emergency kits should provide the necessities of shelter, clothing, food and warmth. Fleece insulation layers, rain jackets, wool socks, matches, flashlight, energy bars and a compact tarp can all be stored in a medium-sized dry bag.

FIRST AID KIT

Paddling often takes us beyond the reach the urban conveniences that make dealing with medical situations quick and easy. First aid kits are an essential part of being prepared for a day out on the water. A good kit needs to be organized, waterproof and easily accessed in an emergency.

First aid kits can be compact and easily stored in a dry bag, dry box or even a wide-mouth Nalgene bottle. Complement your kit with basic first aid training and

A hard-shelled waterproof case is reliable insurance for gear that needs to be protected from water and impact.

WATERPROOF CASES AND DRY BAGS

Canoeing can be a wet sport. Splash, rain or an unplanned dip in the drink can soak valuable camera gear, first aid supplies or spare clothing. Waterproof cases made of high impact plastic and sealed with a rubber "O" ring (such as Pelican cases) are the most reliable and toughest containers for anything that must stay dry. Dry bags are durable sacks most often sealed with a fold-down closure. Reliable and light weight, dry bags are excellent for clothing and soft goods that don't need a hard case for protection.

Water purifiers and filters help ensure you're drinking potable water and allow you to save the substantial weight of carrying extra water in your canoe or over a portage.

WATER AND NUTRITION

Keeping your energy level up requires high energy snacks and lots of water. Paddling all day in hot sun and gentle breezes may sound deceptively easy, but it takes a toll on the body's resources. Take the time to frequently replenish fluids. You will be glad that you did because dehydration is often what makes us feel sluggish and cranky. Without question, if you feel tired and spent in the summer heat, drinking more water will help you feel better.

In addition to carrying adequate water, you may want to bring along a water purifier or water filter. Both will save substantial weight, particularly if you are paddling in a group. With a purifier or filter, you'll have the ability to treat your own water and will be sure to have an ample supply all day long. Efficient in weight and size, some water bottles even come equipped with a filter as part of the bottle assembly.

Energy bars are perhaps the most convenient source of fuel for active people. They contain valuable carbohydrates to replace those used through exertion and are easy to digest while you continue to paddle. Perspiration causes the loss of electrolytes, which need to be replenished. Sport drinks, like Gatorade, help to replace these salts as well as being another source of carbohydrates. Keep in mind that the best overall source of nutrients is a healthy diet containing wholesome foods.

As an alternative to prepared energy bars, you can mix your own high energy trail mix from "good old raisins and peanuts" (GORP). A traditional canoeist's snack food, GORP can be enhanced by other favorite ingredients like chocolate chunks, dried fruits, or anything that will give your system a kick.

SPARE PADDLE

It's rare to lose or break a paddle, but if your partner were to lose their paddle, why give them an opportunity for a free ride home because you weren't carrying a spare? If you are planning to go solo, breaking a paddle could lead to a grim situation at best. For all these very good reasons, a spare paddle is an essential piece of safety equipment. Because it will rarely be used, why not choose an inexpensive spare paddle to keep as a stand-by?

GUIDE BOOKS AND MAPS

Being well-informed is your best insurance for having a safe and enjoyable day on the water. Guide books exist for practically every popular paddling destination accessible by car. A good guide book will have clear route maps, a list of access points, labeled portage routes, points of interest and the nearest roads clearly displayed. Topographical maps are popular choices to provide additional detail about a canoe route. These maps are also handy if you intend to hike as part of the paddling adventure. Look for maps produced at a scale of 1:50 000 because they show a reasonably large area, yet provides enough detail for navigation.

Whenever you are traveling on the water, protect route maps and other essential trip literature in a waterproof chart case. These clear pockets are terrific for protecting maps from water or dirt and can be anchored to the canoe or backpack in windy conditions.

Waterproof chart cases let you to keep your charts and maps out and available for quick reference.

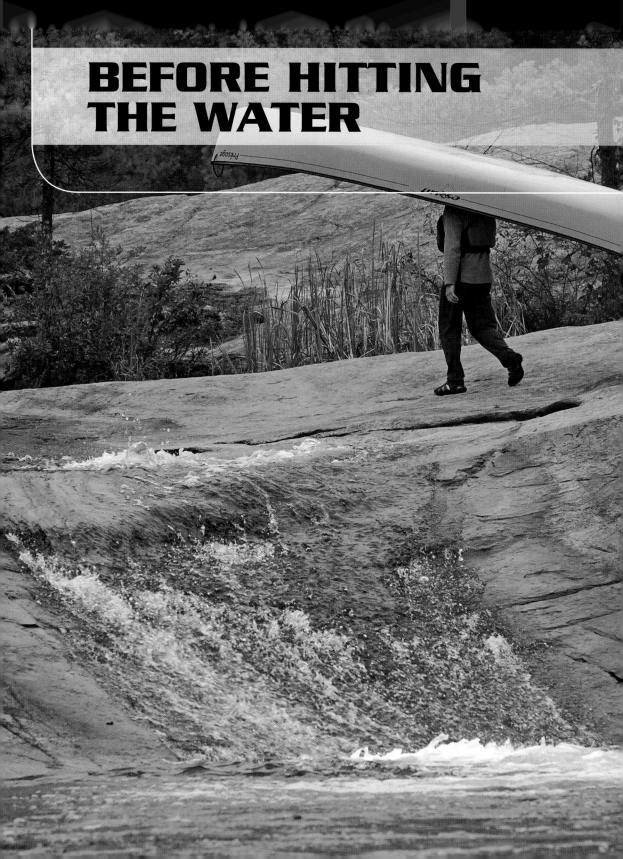

BEFORE HITTING
THE WATER

2

CARING FOR YOUR CANOE

PORTAGING YOUR CANOE

TRANSPORTING YOUR CANOE

GETTING IN AND OUT

PADDLING POSITIONS

Canoes represent a life-long investment. With proper care and storage, canoes will last many decades. Canoes should be stored upside-down, supported by their gunwales. Canoes can be placed on saw horses or hung by ropes from the rafters in a garage or basement. If stored outside, prolonged sun exposure should be avoided because UV rays will make most hull materials brittle. Suspending a tarp above the canoe is an inexpensive method of shading the canoe from direct sunlight. Avoid draping a tarp directly on the hull, because trapped moisture can damage certain finishes on the canoe and accelerate rot in wood gunwales.

Caring for your canoe takes very little time and requires a minimum of additional investment. Many canoes are made of low-maintenance fiberglass, Kevlar, polyester or carbon fiber, as well as plastics like ABS (Royalex). Fiberglass canoes can be cleaned with a mild detergent and a soft cloth. Exterior finishes can be treated with car or boat wax to maintain a glossy appearance. Royalex canoes require a coat of UV protectant to shield the plastic from sun damage and to maintain the finish. Choose products free of petroleum-based additives, like Protectant 303, to avoid both damaging your canoe's finish and leaving an unsightly oil slick the next time you launch your boat.

Wood trim is often used for gunwales and seats in canoes. Common finishes include polyurethane, varnish or oil. Polyurethane and varnished wood coatings need periodic touch-ups to reseal scratches and abrasions. A light sanding and complete re-coating is a good idea every few years. An advantage to oil finishes is that they preserve the wood and are less affected by scratches and abrasion. Oil finishes require more maintenance, and benefit from annual to semi-annual applications of oil to keep the wood looking like new.

Wood and canvas canoes require a modest amount of additional care. Scratches to the painted surface of canvas canoes can be touched up with color-matched paint. The interior of the canoe will need scratches sealed with varnish or polyurethane. Avoid tracking in sand and mud from shoes because the grit eventually settles in between the ribs and planking, adding considerable weight to the hull. Rinsing the interior periodically is a good idea to remove most debris.

PORTAGING YOUR CANOE

The portability of the canoe is what makes canoeing the most versatile means of water transportation. Canoes can be picked up and carried easily to and from the water's edge by just one person. This permits nearly limitless possibilities for paddlers because they can transport their canoe anywhere they wish to paddle. Canoeists create imaginative canoe routes by using portage trails to link lakes and rivers. You can too by simply paddling to the end of a lake, picking up your canoe and walking along a path to the next body of water. Long ago, Native Americans crisscrossed most of North America in just the same way.

Lifting the canoe onto your shoulders is awkward the first few times. If you are paddling tandem, ask your partner to hold the bow of the upside-down canoe over their head as you position yourself beneath the yoke in preparation for the carry. The same teamwork is used to put the canoe down at your destination or when a rest is required. Although two people can also cooperate and carry the canoe together, it is often easier to portage the canoe solo. Try and compare to see which method you prefer.

A nice alternative to carrying your canoe is to use a canoe cart. Although not suited for overly rough terrain, a canoe cart is a quick and efficient means of transporting your canoe when the path is fairly wide and relatively flat.

Lifting a canoe on your own may seem daunting at first. However, there is a trick to the lift that makes it easier than it looks. As with all challenging skills, the one-person lift may take some practice, so choose a level grassy area for your first attempts.

If you are right-handed, approach the canoe on the port side (when facing the bow, this is the left side). If you are left-handed, approach the canoe on the starboard side (the right side when facing the bow). Stand at the center yoke of your upright canoe and grasp the closest gunwales with your hands about shoulder width apart. Bend your knees so that you can lift the canoe onto your thighs. Your legs should now be bearing the weight of the canoe. With a gentle rocking motion, use the leg closest to the bow to heave the far gunwale within grasp of the hand closest to the bow and allow the canoe's weight to settle back onto your bow-side thigh. You are now holding the near gunwale in your stern-side hand, the far gunwale with your bow-side hand, and the canoe's weight is on your bow-side leg. Begin a rocking motion once again, then flip the canoe upward, duck your head a bit, and guide the canoe with your hands over your head to place the yoke onto your shoulders. Do this motion while rotating your stance so that you finish with your body facing the bow.

The solo lift, if completed as described here, does not strain the back because the legs do the lifting. More than that, the legs are actually throwing the canoe above your head! At first this may seem like an unlikely trick, but consider that your leg muscles are powerful enough to let you hop around on one leg, so they are certainly strong enough to support a lightweight canoe.

To put the canoe back down is almost the reverse of the lift. With the canoe level on your shoulders, grip the gunwale with your strongest hand slightly behind the yoke (right if you are right-handed, left if you are left-handed). Your other hand grasps the gunwale ahead of the yoke. Bend at the knees, then gently hop upwards to bounce the canoe up into the air above your shoulders. As the canoe rises, bend at the knees again, keep the far gunwale elevated with your weak hand, and allow your strong hand to lower the canoe down onto your thighs. At the same time, rotate your stance to face to your right as the canoe lands on your legs. Now grip both hands on the closest gunwale and lower the canoe to the ground.

1. Stand at the center yoke. With your hands shoulder-width apart, grab the closest gunwale and tilt the canoe away from you and on its side.

2. Bend your knees. Grabbing the yoke with one hand, lift the canoe onto your thighs.

3. With a gentle rocking motion, use your legs to heave the far gunwale within grasp of your outstretched hand.

4. Once again, with a gentle rocking motion, and with the aid of your legs, flip the canoe upward.

5. Be careful that you don't hit your head on the yoke as you bring the canoe up.

6. Guide the canoe with your hands and place the yoke gently onto your shoulders.

Tandem paddlers who want to portage together can perform the canoe lift as a team. The taller paddler often chooses to lead by carrying the bow, and thus provides better vision to the partner at the stern. Keep in mind the bow carrier has the advantage of better visibility and also has the lighter end of the canoe to carry over the portage.

The tandem lift begins with one paddler at the bow seat and the second at the stern thwart.

Together, stand at the bow and stern of the canoe. Grab the closest gunwale and tilt the canoe on its side, away from you.

Bend your knees and lift the canoe onto your thighs.

As you lift the canoe, turn to face the bow and then guide the bow and stern seats onto your shoulders.

With both paddlers under the canoe it is difficult to see where you are going, so the bow person might want to move further forward to improve visibility.

If the canoe has no stern thwart then the stern seat will do. In unison, both paddlers complete the canoe lift as if they were doing the solo lift. Once the canoe is up above their heads, the bow partner can "walk" their hands towards the bow along the gunwales so that they can rest the bow on their shoulder. The stern person carries the stern thwart (or seat) on their shoulder just as you would a center yoke.

Together, gently rock the canoe, and reach across to the far gunwale. Note that you should both use the same arm (right or left).

Rocking the canoe again, use your legs to launch and lift the canoe over your heads.

To move forward, the bow person hand-walks along the gunwale toward the very front of the canoe.

With the deck plate resting on the bow person's shoulder, it will be much easier to see what's ahead.

TRANSPORTING YOUR CANOE

For safety and convenience when transporting your canoe, use a quality set of roof racks on your vehicle. Although they can be costly, consider the benefits of a quality roof rack system: you will reduce the risk of the canoe falling from your vehicle and becoming a deadly projectile on the highway, the rack will protect the appearance of both your canoe and your car, it's easier to secure the canoe (upside-down down) and you'll have the versatility of a roof rack to carry other items.

When loading canoes onto vehicles, choose a parking area that is level and unobstructed by overhanging trees. Placing the canoe onto your vehicle uses the canoe lift skills covered in the earlier section "Portaging Your Canoe". If you are loading the canoe on your own, position the bow of your canoe near the rear tire of your vehicle. Stand between the vehicle and the canoe and perform a solo canoe lift by holding the canoe near the bow seat. Allow the stern to stay on the ground as you lift the bow above your head. Swing the bow above the vehicle and place it onto

Cam straps are one of the easiest ways to secure a canoe to the roof of your vehicle.

the rear rack bar. Walk to the stern of the canoe, lift and push the canoe onto the vehicle until it is centered on both the front and rear rack bars.

Loading a canoe with a partner uses a tandem canoe lift. Begin beside the vehicle so that once you have lifted the canoe you can proceed to place a gunwale on the rack bars. Finish loading by sliding the canoe across the racks until it is centered on the vehicle. Avoid the temptation to reach across the hood of the vehicle when positioning the canoe. Many backs have missed a day of paddling from the painful "tweak" this awkward reach can cause.

Lashing the canoe to the vehicle requires four 12 foot (3.5 m) lengths of 1 inch (2.5 cm) straps with cam buckles, or four ¾ inch (9 mm) lengths of rope. Two are installed across the hull of the canoe and secured to the roof rack. Two more straps secure the ends of the canoe to the vehicle frame or bumper. Using four straps not only ensures that the canoe is not going to come off the vehicle, but also distributes the wind stress encountered at highway speeds throughout the hull of the canoe.

GETTING IN AND OUT

Canoes are surprisingly stable crafts given that they are rather narrow for their overall length. Stability comes from the way the bottom of the hull is shaped and because the canoe, especially with you in it, has a low center of gravity. In fact, once you are sitting in the canoe, it is actually rather hard to tip it over.

To get in and out of your canoe, choose a suitable location for launching. If you are paddling tandem, one person will hold the canoe while the other gets in. Once in, the kneeling partner can stabilize the canoe while the other partner enters. Docks work very well provided that the height of the dock is similar to the height of the gunwales of the canoe. Docks that are much higher than the canoe require a long step downward before your foot contacts the hull. There is the risk that a misguided foot may upset your balance and send you toppling into the water.

Beaches and shallow shorelines are ideal launching locations because both provide secure footing for that important first step into the boat. If conditions are windy, always point the bow of the boat into the wind. That way, once you begin paddling, you'll be traveling forward into the waves for better control and stability.

When getting in and out of the canoe, remember to maintain a low center of gravity with your feet placed over the centerline of the canoe. Your hands can also hold the paddle across the gunwales in front of your body as a brace for balance.

Working with your partner, grasp the gunwales at midship and slide the canoe along your thighs into the water. Keep the canoe facing bow-first out into the water. The stern person can stabilize the canoe as the bow person enters from the stern. If you are the bow person, place your paddle across the gunwale and push forward as you walk the length of the canoe to reach the bow seat. Place your feet along the centerline of the canoe as you walk. Once at the bow seat, sit down and assume the kneeling position.

To enter the stern, move the canoe a little further from shore before stepping into the boat to avoid grounding the stern on the shore bottom. Similar to your bow partner, place your paddle across the gunwale and slide it forward as you walk ahead of the stern seat and sit down. Lower yourself into a sitting or kneeling position and you are ready to paddle.

Careful launching of your canoe will preserve its beautiful finish and reduce the abrasive wear and tear that can result from sliding it across rough surfaces. Together with a partner, grasp the gunwales so that you are facing each other at the middle of the boat (around the yoke). Lift the canoe up and slide the hull into the water, using your thighs to support the weight of the hull. The person who is to be paddling in the stern will hold the canoe stable next to the dock while the bow person steps in the boat.

To enter at the bow, bend down on the dock adjacent to the bow seat and place the paddle across the gunwales ahead of the seat. Make sure that the paddle blade is on the same side that you'll be paddling. Use your hands to hold both the paddle and the gunwales at the same time. Place one foot into the canoe along the centerline and place the other foot just behind the first. At this point you can either sit or kneel, which will be covered in greater detail in the section entitled Paddling Positions. Either way, spread your knees as wide apart as is comfortable for the most stability.

For the stern entry, the bow person can stabilize the canoe by holding the dock. Getting in at the stern is very similar to the bow entry. Place the paddle across the gunwales ahead of the stern seat with the blade on your paddling side. Step down into the canoe with one foot on the center line and your second foot placed just behind the first. Assume a kneeling position before paddling away from the dock.

With the stern paddler stabilizing the boat from shore, the bow paddler walks up to their seat using the paddle across the gunwales as a brace.

As you become familiar with the feel of canoeing, you may want to experiment with different paddling positions. Canoes have the advantage of permitting a variety of sitting options which can relieve the fatigue associated with holding one position for a long period of time.

Kneeling is the position of choice for increasing canoe stability. Kneeling lowers your center of gravity, which can be a significant safety advantage in windy conditions, or when paddling with children or pets. Sitting on the seat provides welcome relief to sore knees. Some paddlers combine both sitting and kneeling by extending one leg forward while kneeling off the seat. Kneeling also becomes much more comfortable if you have foam pads or something else soft to kneel on.

Kneeling is the most stable position in a canoe, but if you plan to paddle like this, you'll want to have foam pads glued to the floor to protect your knees.

Solo paddlers sit close to the center of the canoe to balance their weight.

If you are paddling a solo canoe, you can sit or kneel as you would in a tandem canoe. However, when paddling solo you typically sit backwards in the bow seat and face the stern of the canoe. This position puts your body weight closer to the center of the canoe, where you have most control. Also, because the canoe is wider in the middle, the canoe will feel more stable.

Paddling solo can also be performed by kneeling in the center of the canoe with your body offset toward your paddling side. Kneeling with the boat tilted to one side is called heeling the canoe. The canoe will take on a pronounced tilt but because you kneel on your heels, your center of gravity will be very low, making for a very stable paddling position. The advantage to paddling with the canoe heeled over is that your paddle strokes are now very close to your body. This permits your strokes to have excellent strength and reach and can make maneuvering the canoe much easier. With practice, you will get a better sense of your balance and can come to feel very comfortable paddling in this position with the boat heeled.

THE ESSENTIALS

THE THREE GOLDEN RULES

PADDLING POSTURE

HOLDING THE PADDLE

CANOE TRIM

THE CANOE IN MOTION

Canoeing, as with any physical activity, can be demanding on your body. Paddling requires you to perform a repeated movement which can cause muscle ache if you are not sufficiently warmed up. By knowing your body's strength, endurance and flexibility, you can budget your level of activity to avoid muscle and joint injury. Prepare your muscles and joints before going canoeing, and you can reduce the risk of soreness after a great day on the water.

Judged by appearances, canoeing can look as if the arms do most of the work. It may come as a surprise that the torso actually provides the "driving" force in propelling the canoe forward. Typically this is a very strong region of the body for most healthy people, so much of the strength needed for canoeing is already inside you. You can continue to build on this "power" by strengthening and toning the torso muscles through exercise like Pilates or yoga. The results will not only give you better posture, but it will make canoeing easier and also assist you when balancing your canoe.

Canoeing is not often associated with endurance sports like marathon running, cycling or swimming. Of course, if you are quietly stroking your canoe through a moose pond looking for wildlife, paddling may not be all that physically demanding. Yet, if you imagine paddling all day long on an extended wilderness canoe trip with heavy packs weighing down your boat, then the physical demands will be quite different. This sort of participation requires some advance preparation so that your body is ready for what lies ahead. Proper conditioning can include short daytrips before a long excursion. Similarly, running or cycling provides cross-training benefits to prepare your cardiovascular system for the rigors of extended canoe trips with strenuous portages. It's more fun to be up for the match when we plan any type of physical activity, so judge your endurance level wisely and be prepared to meet the challenge.

Prepare yourself for paddling by spending a few minutes warming up with light physical activity and some key stretches. Stretching can increase your range of motion and may reduce the risk of soreness and injury. Just as important are follow-up stretches. These should be completed after canoeing, or before a long rest break, and will help keep joints limber to reduce possible muscle stiffness.

Paddling requires an active upper body. Stretching shoulders, neck and chest muscles will allow freer movement of your arms and paddle, and make the placement of strokes easier. Loosening the upper and lower back, and stretching your sides will help you access the power in your torso muscles for forward propulsion, both for gentle cruising and for those times when you need a little extra power. Finally, include the legs in your stretching routine. The legs help anchor the activity of the torso firmly to the hull, especially in the kneeling position. Pay close special attention to calf and hamstring muscles.

Adopting a good stretching regime like yoga
keeps the body limber and reduces the risk of injury.

THE THREE GOLDEN RULES

Canoeing comfortably is an exercise in stability, much the same way cycling works because of balance. The "Three Golden Rules" will focus your attention on moving your canoe with poise and confidence, whether paddling tandem or solo—even when the winds are high and the lake is rough. These rules will help you manage your center of gravity so that the canoe remains stable, enabling you to paddle with ease, finesse and strength.

The lower body moves with the boat, while the head and upper body maintain balance.

KEEP YOUR UPPER AND LOWER BODY INDEPENDENT

The upper and lower bodies have vital, yet unique roles to play when paddling the canoe. The upper body controls the paddle and ultimately provides most of the power needed to propel your canoe. The lower body is in charge of boat tilt which is a necessary component of stability and is also used for carving effective turns.

Although your paddle is gripped by your hands, it is really the upper body that provides the majority of the strength needed to power each and every stroke. Think of the arms as the mechanism required to hold the paddle and for tuning its position in the water, while your torso is the motor that drives each stroke through to completion.

While the upper body is concerned with the paddle and balance, the lower body is actively holding the canoe to give you good boat control. This is accomplished by pressing the knees against the floor of the canoe, and by resting your buttocks on the seat. It's easy to think that the lower body is just along for the ride, but this is far from the truth. Good boat control results from actively using your lower body to hold and guide the canoe on its intended path. For example, during canoe turns you need to hold the canoe on a tilt to get the best response. The lower body flexes at the hip to allow a knee to push down against the hull. This movement creates boat tilt, which helps maximize the turning performance of the canoe.

Orchestrating the movement of both upper and lower body in harmony to control both paddle and boat is the art of canoeing.

2 ROTATE YOUR TORSO

Rotating your torso on every paddle stroke engages the large core muscle groups and adds considerable strength to your canoeing technique. Rotation also taps into your strong leg muscles which anchor your movements to the canoe hull through the contact points of buttocks and knees. Torso rotation makes use of the entire body to provide thrust behind every paddle stroke.

Torso rotation begins with the extension of the arm and shoulder on the side that you are paddling on. This movement results in the twisting and tensioning of your upper body. This twist is also referred to as the wind-up—think of it as the preparation phase for a stroke. After the wind-up, the paddle is placed in the water ready to begin the desired stroke. The power phase is performed by unwinding the torso and unleashing the torque of the large core muscles. Stroke completion usually sees the hip advance toward the paddle and has the torso assuming its natural forward facing stance.

Each stroke involves a full body work-out. The arms play the essential role of positioning the paddle for the stroke, the hands guide the paddle through the stroke movement and the unwinding of the large torso muscles provides the power to propel the canoe.

Torso rotation makes use of the entire body, giving strength and precision to each stroke.

To keep your hands within your field of vision while taking a stroke behind you, you need to turn your upper body and head fairly aggressively.

Keeping your arms within your field of vision permits stronger paddle strokes. This is because the arms are most powerful when they perform work in front of the body. When the paddle is placed in the water for a stroke, the arms are said to be in the "power position" only if they are positioned in front of a vertical plane created by your shoulders. Any reach that causes the arms to move behind the shoulders will greatly reduce your strength and will make paddling more difficult.

Maintaining the arms within your field of vision will also limit how high you may reach with your grip hand. This is good because extending the upper hand too far above the head can make

paddle strokes awkward. By keeping your hand within sight you will be able to link strokes with greater ease and develop less fatigue. You can also blend different strokes into one another more smoothly when your arms remain within your field of vision.

Safety is another point to consider with regard to arm position. Although shoulder injuries are rare in flat water canoeing, overuse and joint strain may result from poor technique. Over extension of the arms, reaching behind the shoulder or above the head, can all leave the joint vulnerable to injury. Good technique should always have your hands and arms positioned within your field of vision.

PADDLING POSTURE

Proper posture improves your paddling strokes and maintains your balance in the canoe.

Sitting in your canoe with good posture benefits both your sense of balance and your back comfort. Boat control and paddling performance are all affected by body posture because, in a canoe, body leans in any direction will affect how the boat floats on the water. In most circumstances, paddling requires that you sit with a relaxed upright posture.

Sitting at the midpoint of the seat with an upright posture centers your body weight over the keel or centerline of the canoe. This balanced position is your best posture for maintaining stability, especially when paddling through waves, or when an unexpected weight shift occurs, such as the sudden movement of your paddling partner as they reach for a camera or water bottle.

An erect paddling posture takes pressure off the legs so they can be used to tilt the hull during changes in traveling direction. When canoes are turned left or right, they are tilted toward the direction of the turn much like a bicycle is leaned as it goes around a corner. Unlike cycling however, it is not necessary to lean your body when canoeing. Only the boat is tilted, and this is done by pushing one of your knees down, but keeping your torso centered.

Tilting the canoe with your legs allows you to keep your body upright and in a stable and comfortable position. With most of your weight supported on the canoe seat, the legs are free to move up and down to adjust boat tilt. Keeping the legs loose also allows the canoe to roll with waves whenever they approach from the side.

HOLDING THE PADDLE

A tight grip is not necessary. Hold your paddle with a relaxed grasp and loose, flexible wrists. This will allow your hands and arms to move freely and execute fluid paddle strokes. All strokes should flow together with an ease that makes the end of one stroke indistinguishable from the beginning of the next.

When holding the paddle, the hand which holds the shaft is called the shaft hand and the hand grasping the paddle grip is the control hand. To locate where to hold the shaft, place the paddle grip under your armpit, drape your arm down the shaft and extend your thumb so it is pointed at the paddle blade. Next, grip the paddle with your other hand just beneath your extended thumb. This will be the location of your shaft hand when you're paddling. If your paddle is of the right length, there should be 4 to 5 inches between your hand and the throat of the paddle blade.

During forward strokes, the face of the blade that pulls the water toward you is called the power face and the reverse side is called the back face. The control hand manages how the faces are used in a stroke. Control of the faces is accomplished by bending your wrist towards or away from you, which twists the paddle shaft and blade. The shaft hand helps the control hand by holding the paddle shaft in the correct position for a stroke. The shaft hand allows the shaft to turn freely within its grasp while the control hand twists the paddle as required for whatever stroke is being performed.

Once seated in the canoe, the side on which you are paddling is referred to as your on-side. The opposite side of the canoe is likewise labeled your off-side. This is standard "canoe talk", and replaces the descriptors "left" and "right".

Choosing a side on which to paddle really comes down to personal comfort. In tandem canoes, paddling partners must paddle on opposite sides of the canoe in order to equalize the force of their strokes and to keep the canoe balanced. Switching sides in the early stages of learning may delay the acquisition of your skills and lead to unnecessary frustration. Although it's tempting for the solo canoeist to swap sides for various maneuvers, this too is generally frowned upon. This is because switching sides as a defensive response to a situation will often compromise balance.

As your paddling skills develop, the ability to paddle on both sides will be a significant asset. For those who have mastered strokes on both sides of the canoe, alternating sides on longer outings can relieve fatigue that sets in after stroking on just one side of the canoe for long periods of time. Of course, those who are lucky enough to be ambidextrous will enjoy being able to team up with other paddlers regardless of their partner's preferred paddling side.

1. Place the paddle grip snugly under your armpit. Grasp the
   paddle shaft with a straight arm and with your thumb extended.

2. Place your shaft hand beneath your thumb on the paddle shaft.

3. You've now found the ideal position for your hands on your paddle.

CANOE TRIM

Trimming a canoe refers to balancing the weight carried in the boat. There are two ways to trim: left to right, and bow to stern. It is always preferable to balance the weight of people and gear equally left to right in a canoe. This maximizes the seaworthiness of the canoe and makes it stable. Trimming bow to stern should result in the canoe riding nearly flat in the water, although it is acceptable to have the stern resting a little lower in the water than the bow.

The act of trimming may be accomplished by simply experimenting with the location of gear being carried until you are satisfied with the balance of the canoe. Some canoe models come equipped with a sliding bow seat. The seat is used to adjust trim by allowing the bow partner to move forward or backward as required to level the boat.

THE CANOE IN MOTION

Whether traveling on land, sea or air, few vehicles rival the beauty and function of the canoe. The ease with which canoes can be paddled and maneuvered across lakes and down rivers, even when heavily loaded, is testament to the efficiency of the classic canoe. Hidden within this unique shape lies the secret of the canoe's success.

Picture the canoe's pointed bow piercing the water like an arrowhead as you paddle across a lake. As the boat moves forward, the bow splits the water apart to make way for the passing of the canoe. Water pressure builds up on either side of the canoe and as a result, small waves emerge along the hull from the bow to the mid-point of the hull. Past the middle of the canoe and toward the stern, the shape of the boat narrows, creating a vacuum that is indicated by the absence of waves.

What this means is that as the canoe moves forward, the bow is pinned by the frontal resistance of the approaching water, and the stern is free to move side-to-side because it glides along without restriction. The magic of the canoe lies in this contrast of resistance. The bow's streamlined shape allows the canoe to travel with great efficiency, and the stern's freedom to move side-to-side permits easy maneuverability. This is why steering is usually performed at the stern.

It's important to note that bow paddlers can only provide assisting turning strokes after the turn has been initiated by the stern paddler.

The same order of stroke execution is performed by the solo paddler. Stern strokes are executed first to initiate a change of direction, and then followed by bow strokes to assist and control the remainder of the turn.

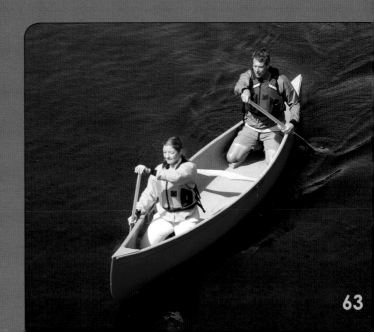

A well trimmed canoe makes paddling almost effortless!

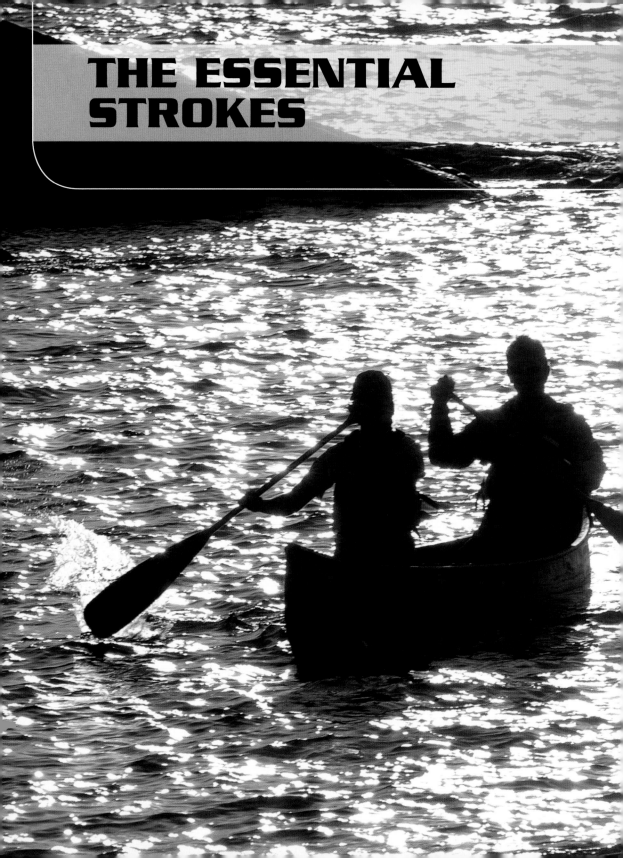

THE ESSENTIAL STROKES

4

FORWARD STROKES

REVERSE STROKES

TURNING STROKES

LATERAL STROKES

STABILITY STROKES

Proficiency in sport requires learning new skills that combine coordination and timing. For many, the initial stages of learning can feel a little awkward. Learning to paddle a canoe may seem frustrating at first, but take heart, with repetition it will get easier. As you practice, and continuously repeat the same movements, you will develop muscle memory. Eventually, your muscles will remember how to do each stroke, and you will no longer be burdened with thinking about coordination or timing.

There are useful language conventions to help with the discussion of strokes. These terms were introduced in the section, Holding the Paddle. To review: when referring to the different faces of a paddle, the power face is the side of the blade that pulls water, and the back face is the reverse side. Strokes performed on your own paddling side are called your on-side strokes, and those on the opposite side are called your off-side strokes. To refer to the turning side of a tandem canoe, the boat's on-side and off-side are the same as the bow paddler's.

In tandem canoeing, it is most effective for both paddlers to paddle in unison. Each stroke taken by the bow person is matched by a complementary stroke taken at the same time in the stern. The bow paddler sets the paddling pace because it is easier for the stern partner to watch the cadence of the person in the bow, and then match them stroke-for-stroke. In solo canoes, paddlers try to keep an even timing between strokes as if following a musical beat. (This is not such an odd notion, really, since Voyageurs used songs to synchronize their strokes when paddling along trade routes.)

A number of factors can influence the performance of your strokes. For example, different canoe models have distinctive characteristics which may cause them to require a fewer or greater number of strokes to achieve certain maneuvers. Of course there are variations in people too. Since not all people have equal abilities, strokes may have to be adapted to match a person's level of fitness and/or flexibility. The good news is that in canoeing, less-than-perfect strokes will still get the job done, so there is no need to be hard on yourself or a well-intentioned partner.

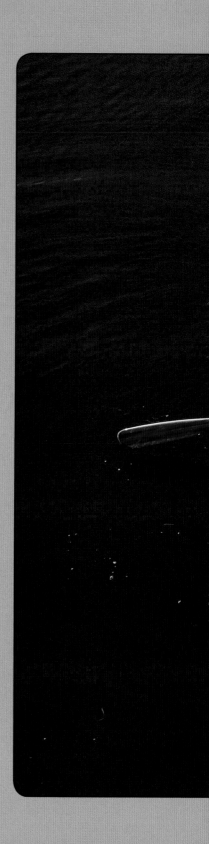

In this case, the solo canoeist's on-side is on the left, while the on-side for the tandem canoe is on the right—the on-side of the bow paddler.

FORWARD STROKES

The majority of movement in a canoe involves forward motion of some kind. Even when turning a corner, the canoe is still moving forward. This is why propulsion strokes are so important. By maximizing your efficiency, you'll avoid tired arm muscles and be able to enjoy a full day on the water.

Forward strokes can be quickly and easily learned by anyone new to canoeing, but there are more complex refinements that can be learned to optimize your efficiency. Canoeing is a little like chess: full mastery takes a long time, but with a little instruction you can really enjoy the game. In the end, well practiced strokes will provide the control necessary to allow you to silently creep up on moose feeding in the shallows, or wind your way along sinuous rivers.

FORWARD STROKE

Enjoyable and efficient paddling depends more on the merits of a good forward stroke than on any other paddling skill. Superior technique exploits the large muscle groups in your body, helping you avoid muscle fatigue and strain. A well-executed forward stroke looks and feels graceful and fluid, the whole body moving in harmony.

As with all the propulsion strokes, the forward stroke requires the "Three Golden Rules": an independent upper and lower body, good torso rotation, and hands positioned within your field of view. As mentioned before, torso rotation is the key to creating the most powerful stroke with minimal fatigue by using all of your body's major muscle groups.

The level of physical exertion required for the forward stroke should roughly equal that used for walking. If you feel comfortable walking long distances, then canoeing for sustained periods should not feel any more onerous.

Although you can just dip your paddle in and pull it through the water any way you like, you're probably reading this book because you are curious about the possible refinements. With that said, we're going to look at the ideal forward stroke—one which will power your canoe forward the most effectively. Whether you are out for a relaxed, casual paddle, or racing to the finish line, your forward stroke should always include the same four elements—you choose the level of intensity with which they are applied: wind-up, catch, power phase, and recovery.

Although most canoeists will adopt a relaxed forward stroke that promotes endurance, we're going to look at a highly efficient forward stroke, as the key elements for both are the same.

WIND-UP

The wind-up twists the upper body in preparation for the power phases of the stroke and is crucial for engaging the torso muscles for a powerful and efficient stroke. Throughout the wind-up, the paddle is held above the water. As you swing the paddle into position toward the bow, twist the paddle with your control hand thumb forward so that the blade slices through the air edge first, which minimizes the wind resistance upon it.

When slicing your blade foward, rotate your torso so that your shaft hand extends toward the bow of the canoe. Keep your shaft arm straight with your hand just above the on-side gunwale. Place your control arm in front of your forehead with the elbow slightly bent. As with the shaft hand, the control hand should be nearly over your on-side gunwale. Remember to keep both arms within your field of vision.

A successful and relaxed stroke also relies on maintaining a comfortable body posture, so only rotate within your range of comfort.

CATCH

The catch occurs when the paddle enters and grabs the water. A good catch has hardly any splash or sound. As your arms lower the paddle into the water, check that the angle of the blade is perpendicular to the gunwale. During the catch, the shaft hand begins its movement sternward alongside the gunwale while the control hand pushes toward the bow. The catch builds water pressure on the blade, and it should feel almost as though your paddle is anchored in something solid. With the paddle anchored by the catch, the forward stroke will have the necessary traction and avoid paddle slippage.

---

1. Rotating your torso, or "winding up" as you plant your stroke lets you reach further toward the bow and engages your torso muscles for the stroke.

2. For the catch, plant your blade deeply in the water, causing as little splash as possible.

3. Power for the stroke comes from unwinding your torso, pulling on the shaft hand, and pushing with the control hand.

4. The power phase of the stroke ends when the blade is in line with your knee.

5. Lift the paddle out of the water by slicing it out to the side.

6. With the blade clear of the water, lead it edge first toward the bow for the next stroke.

1

2

3

4

5

6

1. During the wind-up, the torso is twisted to engage the back and abdominal muscles.

2. For maximum forward propulsion, the paddle shaft is vertical during the power phase of the stroke.

3. When the stroke finishes at your knee, slice the blade out of the water by twisting the thumb of your control hand forward as it drops across your body.

POWER PHASE

Throughout the power phase it is helpful to picture the effect of the forward stroke. Although it may seem counter-intuitive, think of it this way: the paddle is not pulled backward through the water—rather, the canoe is propelled forward toward the paddle.

During the wind-up, you rotated your torso so that your on-side shoulder was pointing towards the bow, with the paddle well ahead of your body. In the power phase, you will uncoil your upper body, pulling your body forward toward the anchored paddle. In this step it is important to let the torso muscles do the work. If you try to pull with only your arms, the stroke will be weaker and you'll get tired faster. As you uncoil your body, use your control hand to apply forward pressure on the paddle grip, using the paddle much like a lever where your shaft hand acts as the fulcrum or pivot point.

As you unwind your torso, the canoe moves forward against the resistance of the anchored paddle until your knees reach your shaft hand. At the end of the stroke, your paddle shaft should be vertical with your hands stacked one above the other, and your shoulders should be lined up perpendicular to the gunwales. This completes the torso rotation and the power phase. Resist the temptation to continue the power phase past the knees because this will over-rotate your torso and decrease the efficiency of the stroke.

Remember that the power of the forward stroke comes from your body's largest muscles located in your torso. By unwinding the torso from its twisted position you will incorporate abdominal, back and even leg muscles, into the power phase of the forward stroke. The more rotation provided to a stroke, the more power it will have. Allow your arms to simply tune the paddle's position throughout the stroke.

EXIT

The exit occurs in the span between your knees and hips. Lift the paddle from the water and ready it for the return swing forward to link it to the wind-up of the next stroke. To exit the blade, use both hands to lift the paddle from the water. During the exit, as your shaft hand approaches your hip, arc it outward over the water while you let your control hand move slightly toward the middle of the canoe from its position over the gunwale. Remove the blade from the water adjacent to the hip, and twist your control hand at the wrist to point its thumb forward. The blade slices through the air, edge first, as you begin the wind-up of the next forward stroke.

J STROKE

The J stroke is a version of the forward stroke that is used only by tandem stern and solo paddlers. Its purpose is to keep the canoe going in a straight line, while still providing forward momentum. It is necessary because every forward stroke turns the canoe a little to the stern or solo paddler's off-side. The J stroke adds a small pry at the end of the power phase of the forward stroke, and is only effective for a person in the back half of the canoe.

   The J portion of the stroke comes after you have completed the power phase of the forward stroke and essentially replaces the exit. The J motion is created by prying off the gunwale as the paddle passes from knee to hip. The "J" name comes from the supposed shape the paddle carves in the water—straight along the gunwale then hooked outward to the side. This J is more an illusion than a reality—remember that it is really the canoe that moves through the water, not the paddle.

1 As the forward stroke ends, the J-stroke begins—with the control hand above the gunwale and the shaft hand anchored at the hip.

To perform the j stroke, complete the wind-up, catch and power phase as you would for the forward stroke. Once your paddle shaft is adjacent to your knee, you are ready to begin the prying motion off the gunwale. To start the pry, twist your control hand so that its thumb points toward the bow of the boat. This movement will twist the power face away from the canoe. Allow the paddle shaft to rotate in the grasp of your shaft hand by keeping a fairly loose grip on the paddle.

Use your control hand to pull the paddle grip inward and re-position your hand above the on-side knee. This inward movement has the effect of prying the blade off the gunwale and away from the canoe. While you are doing this, use your shaft hand to brace the paddle shaft on the gunwale close to, but still ahead of, the hip. This movement uses the paddle like a lever, where the gunwale is the fulcrum or pivot point.

Twist the control hand's thumb forward and down while you pull the control hand inward. This movement will pry the blade out off the canoe's gunwale.

75

CROSS FORWARD STROKE

1 **2** **3**

Due to the awkward arm position, you'll get the most power for the cross forward stroke by leaning forward to plant your paddle, and then thrusting your hips forward as you take the stroke.

The cross forward stroke is one of the most helpful strokes used by solo canoeists. It's often used in combination with a regular forward stroke to accelerate the canoe forward from a stand-still, because it counters the forward stroke's tendency to veer the canoe toward the off-side during starts. By stroking on both sides of the canoe at start-up, you can balance your strokes side-to-side and accelerate in a straight line.

This stroke can also be used in place of a forward stroke when paddling around a curve to your off-side. For best results though, don't look to win a race with the cross forward; it is a slow to mid-speed stroke.

For a powerful stroke, bend forward to plant the paddle toward the bow on the off-side of the canoe. The power of this stroke comes from thrusting the hips forward toward the paddle. The strength of your hip thrust is determined by how far you bend forward at the outset. A variation of the stroke is used when the canoe is already moving. Because the hip thrust is such a slow movement, you can opt to do the stroke with just the arms. Though weaker, stroking with just arms is fast enough to keep up with a moving canoe as it carves around a bend to your off-side.

The cross forward begins with the paddle lifted

4 **5** **6**

*The stroke ends at your knee, at which time you'll twist
your control hand 90 degrees thumb forward so that
you can slice the blade back to where it started.*

across the canoe and submerged in the water adjacent to the hull on the off-side. Bend forward at the waist to increase your reach and to enable the hips to add power to the stroke. Your control hand should reach just beyond your knee and the shaft hand should reach even further toward the bow. Both hands should be over the gunwale.

The power phase comes from thrusting the hips forward toward the paddle. A hip thrust resembles the same motion you would use if you were sitting in a chair that you wanted to move closer to the kitchen table. As the stroke progresses, use your control hand to push the paddle grip forward while you use your shaft hand

to pull the paddle into a vertical position. Both hands finish the stroke near the knee. Similar to the forward stroke, during the cross forward it is the canoe that moves ahead, as opposed to the paddle being pulled backward.

For the recovery, twist your control hand thumb a quarter-turn to point it toward the bow. This rotates the blade's power face toward the hull so that you can lift the paddle edge-first out of the water and back over to your on-side. Alternatively, you may decide to turn and slice the blade along the hull, keeping it in the water, and return it to the starting position of another cross forward stroke.

Paddling backward is a convenient way to do things like back away from shore, or move away from a dock. Back paddling relies on many of the same elements as the forward stroke, such as aligning your hands over the gunwale, using torso rotation for added power, and maintaining an even cadence with your bow partner.

BACK STROKE

As with the forward stroke, there are four progressive steps to the back stroke: wind-up, catch, power phase and exit. Linked together, these steps can appear as smooth and graceful as the forward stroke. Although not used as frequently, the back stroke can be very helpful in maneuvering in tighter environments like rocky shorelines.

Begin the back stroke by rotating the torso so that your on-side shoulder points toward the stern. As with the forward stroke, the wind-up allows you to tap into the strong torso muscles that help propel the canoe.

With the completion of the wind-up, the paddle should be alongside the canoe with the blade pointing toward the stern. Begin the catch by pushing the blade's back face down into the water with the shaft hand while at the same time progressively pulling upward on the grip. As the paddle becomes vertical unwind at the hips to add power to the stroke.

Throughout the power phase, the paddle shaft rides along the hull beside the gunwale with the shaft hand at or above gunwale height. Unwind your torso until your on-side shoulder has rotated to a position that points to your on-side knee and your shaft arm is fully extended. The control arm continues to reach over the gunwale to keep the paddle blade beside the hull.

The exit is simple enough: you just lift the paddle straight up out of the water. To link one backstroke to another, arc the shaft hand backward over the water and drop the control hand to chest level. This movement will rotate your body and paddle back toward the stern and wind you up for your next stroke.

1. Wind up for the backstroke by rotating your torso towards the paddle.

2. With the blade planted fully in the water, aggressively unwind the body while pushing forward with the shaft hand and pulling with the control hand.

3. The power phase continues until your shoulders are again square with the gunwales.

4. Simply lift the blade out of the water during the exit phase.

CROSS BACK STROKE

In solo canoes, you can move backward in a straight line by alternating back strokes and cross back strokes. These two strokes are used much the same way as forward and cross forward strokes are used to accelerate the solo canoe forward.

The cross back begins by lifting the paddle across the canoe to the off-side and placing it in the water as far behind your hip as possible. Good torso rotation is the key to achieve this catch position. Place the paddle in the water vertically with the power face ready to pull the water for the power phase.

1. Lower your control hand to position the paddle horizontally in front of your body.

2. Rotate your torso and swing your shaft hand across the canoe.

3. Only aggressive torso rotation will make it possible to plant your stroke beside or behind your hip.

4. Plant the paddle deeply in the water beside your off-side hip with the shaft held as vertically as possible.

5. Unwind your torso and pull the paddle toward the bow.

6. Keep the stroke short and sweet.

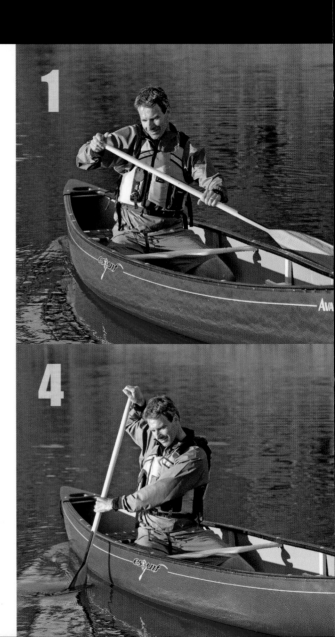

Paddling backward requires a role reversal for tandem paddlers. The bow person takes control of steering with the reverse J-stroke, while the stern paddler maintains the momentum.

REVERSE J STROKE

The reverse J stroke combines the power of the back stroke with the directional control offered by a pry at the bow. Reverse J strokes are used for course correction by both solo, and the bow paddler in a tandem canoe. As the canoe moves backward, the reverse J stroke counters the effect of veering away from your paddle side as a result of the back stroke.

To do the reverse J stroke, complete the reverse stroke's usual wind-up, catch and power phases. When the paddle has been extended toward the bow insert a small pry off the gunwale before the exit phase of the reverse stroke. To initiate the pry, turn your control hand thumb down, which will position the back face of the paddle blade away from the canoe. Pry by pulling the control hand inboard over the on-side knee. This pry will turn the stern toward your on-side.

TURNING STROKES

FORWARD SWEEP

A stroke for solo canoeists, the forward sweep takes the paddle on an arcing path from the bow to the stern of the canoe and turns the boat toward your off-side. The forward sweep begins with the blade placed in the water at the bow, power face outward. Keep your control hand in front of your stomach and the shaft arm fully extended. Twist at the waist to assist your shaft arm's reach. To sweep, hold your arms rigid and rotate your torso so that the paddle arcs from the bow to the stern.

You will notice that when the paddle is firmly planted in the water that the canoe actually pivots around the anchored paddle. The torso muscles do all the work of moving the canoe, and your hands and arms simply maintain the proper paddle position throughout the stroke.

Twisting at the torso, reach the shaft arm as far forward as possible and plant your paddle near the bow of the canoe.

Sweep as wide an arc as possible out to the side of the canoe while keeping your control hand low and in front of your stomach.

Power for the stroke comes from unwinding at the waist. Let the torso muscles do the work.

Following the movement of the paddle with your eyes encourages torso rotation—which provides the most power for the stroke.

The stroke ends just before your blade hits the stern, having completed a sweep of almost 180 degrees.

85

1 The reverse sweep is initiated at the stern of the canoe with an aggressive torso rotation and the control hand held low and in front of the stomach.

2 Unwind your torso and sweep a wide arc out to the side with the paddle, keeping your hands low.

3 Notice the arms stay in a relatively fixed position throughout the sweep, clearly indicating that torso rotation provides most of the power for the stroke.

4 The stroke ends at the bow, having completed a sweep of almost 180 degrees.

REVERSE SWEEP

The reverse sweep spins a solo canoe around its center axis or pivot point. This stroke is very effective because your sitting position (and your center of gravity) is almost directly above the boat's pivot point. Because you'll have to twist your torso fairly aggressively from back to front, good flexibility is definitely an asset for this stroke!

As a solo paddler, you have the advantage of sitting at the mid-point of the canoe where you can easily reach either end of the boat with your paddle. From the middle of the canoe, you can complete a sweep where the blade spans the distance from stern to bow. The effect is pretty amazing—you can spin the canoe in a complete circle with just two strokes!

The reverse sweep starts with a full torso rotation so that your shoulders face the on-side gunwale. Reach the paddle toward the stern with your control hand at stomach level and your shaft hand extended behind your hip. The paddle begins the stroke as close to the hull as possible. While unwinding your upper body, sweep the paddle in a wide arc out to the side of the canoe and all the way around to the bow. When done correctly, there is practically no movement of the arms because the torso does all the work. Lift the paddle clear at the bow before the canoe overrides the blade, which can cause you to "trip" on the stroke. Return to your normal paddling posture ready for the next stroke.

The stationary bow draw is different from the draw stroke described in the upcoming section Lateral Strokes. It is one of the assistive strokes used by the bow person to help turn a moving canoe to the on-side, but it can also be used by a solo paddler to turn a canoe. Carried by the forward momentum of the moving canoe, the blade cuts into the approaching water and creates the resistance needed to pull the canoe around in an arc.

Think of the stationary bow draw as a bow rudder. Initially, the stroke is held with the paddle motionless in the water. The stroke uses the blade edge to lead the canoe into the arc of a turn. The rudder effect is increased by opening the blade angle, or decreased by lessening the blade angle. As long as the paddle is held in a vertical position, changing the blade angle will steer the canoe with surprising accuracy.

The stationary bow draw starts with the paddle placed in the water to the side of the canoe just ahead of your knee. For the best performance, hold the paddle shaft as vertically as possible. To make the reach more comfortable and to provide the necessary power for the stroke, rotate your torso slightly to face the paddle. Your shaft arm can remain bent at the elbow and your control arm extends outward in front of your forehead.

Twist the paddle shaft with your control hand so that the leading edge of the blade is pointed into the direction of the turn. The direction of the twist should cause your control thumb to point toward your forehead. Be prepared to brace the position of the paddle by tightening your torso muscles against the resistance felt on the blade as it gets pulled to your on-side.

You can add to the turning effect of this stroke by drawing (pulling) the paddle to the side of the canoe, making it a bow draw instead of a stationary bow draw. As you do so, gradually turn the blade so it finishes with the power face parallel to the hull instead of at an open angle. Additional draws can be added by doing a slice recovery to link each stroke. Turn your control thumb away from the canoe to twist the blade perpendicular to the gunwales. Using a slice, reposition the paddle away from the canoe, then turn the blade parallel to the hull and draw back to the side of the canoe. With each draw, continue to wind and unwind your torso for added power and to avoid straining your back.

The stationary bow draw acts much like a "bow rudder". Just point the leading edge of the paddle in the direction you wish to travel and let the force of the water pull you around the turn. Notice the torso is rotated to face the paddle.

The cross bow draw involves aggressive torso rotation that keeps the paddle in front of your body.

CROSS BOW DRAW

The cross bow draw is a powerful stroke to maneuver a solo or tandem canoe toward your off-side. Although belonging to the family of draw strokes, the cross bow is often used when the canoe is moving forward and is adapted to act as a bow rudder. Used as a rudder, the paddle is held with the leading edge directed into the approaching water as the canoe arcs around a bend. The cross bow draw assists the turn by pulling the bow further into the curve and can be used much like a steering wheel—simply by increasing or decreasing the angle of the blade, you can control the tightness of the turn.

Start by lifting the paddle over the canoe to the off-side and planting it in the water away from the canoe and just in front of your knee position. Rotate at the hips at the same time to achieve good paddle placement and to prepare the torso to power the stroke. The control hand and the shaft hand are stacked one over the other to create a vertical paddle shaft.

Use your control hand to twist the paddle grip and aim the paddle blade away from the canoe in the direction of the turn. The direction of twist means your control thumb will point away from the canoe. The cross bow draw's effect can be increased by pulling the paddle to the canoe. For repeated cross draws, point your thumb inward to permit slicing the blade away from the canoe to re-position the paddle.

STERN PRY

The stern pry is a great stroke for initiating turns toward the solo canoe's on-side or a tandem canoe's off-side. The stern pry is different from the standard pry described in the upcoming section Lateral Strokes as the paddle is held horizontally, not vertically. Also, the stern pry works in combination with the forward stroke. The momentum provided by the forward stroke helps to drive the canoe around a bend.

The set up for the stern pry begins at the end of the power phase of the forward stroke where the paddle is vertical, and adjacent to the knee. From here, slice the paddle along the hull by twisting the grip with the control hand so that your thumb points toward the stern. Position the paddle parallel to the canoe, with your shaft hand braced on the gunwale at the hip. The control hand should be in line with the on-side knee and held just outside of the gunwale. Twist your shoulders to the on-side to keep the paddle within your field of view.

Apply power to the paddle by untwisting your torso and pry the paddle shaft against the gunwale. For extra leverage, you can pull the control hand as far as the on-side knee. This moves the blade away from the hull, pushes the stern away from your paddle, and starts the canoe into an on-side turn. Once the stroke is completed, swing the paddle forward to ready it for another forward stroke and perhaps another stern draw if it's required.

1 The pry starts with your paddle flat against the side of the canoe at the stern, with your shaft hand resting on the gunwale just behind the hip and your control hand reaching across the canoe.

2 Pull the control hand inward while your shaft hand stays on the gunwale, acting as a pivot point for the pry.

STERN DRAW

When moving forward, the stern draw is one of the steering strokes used to initiate a canoe turn. The stern draw varies from the regular draw, described in the next section, in that the paddle is held nearly horizontally, rather than vertically. Since the stern draw is used when the canoe is in motion, it is necessary to link it to a forward stroke. The forward stroke helps to maintain canoe momentum throughout the turn.

Once you have completed the power phase of the forward stroke, the paddle will be at your knee. From here, set-up the stern draw by twisting your control hand slightly to point the blade towards the stern at a 45 degree angle to the centerline of the canoe. Slice the paddle behind your back but still pointing away from the canoe. Your shaft hand should be extended over the water behind your hip and your control hand just behind the on-side knee. The paddle will now be almost horizontal.

Begin the stern draw with your shoulders perpendicular to the gunwale, and then twist your upper body toward the stern, moving the paddle to the hull as you twist. Push the control hand out over the water during the torso twist to strengthen the drawing force of the stroke. Just before the paddle makes contact with the side of the canoe, lift it from the water so that you can avoid "tripping" on the stroke, or getting the paddle caught under the hull. Next, either swing the paddle in front of the body, ready for another forward stroke, or repeat the stern draw if necessary.

1. With your control hand above your on-side knee, plant the paddle out and away from the canoe at about 45 degrees to the gunwales.

2. With your control hand, plant the paddle out and away from the canoe at about 45 degrees to the gunwales.

3. Finish the stroke by punching your control hand out over the water.

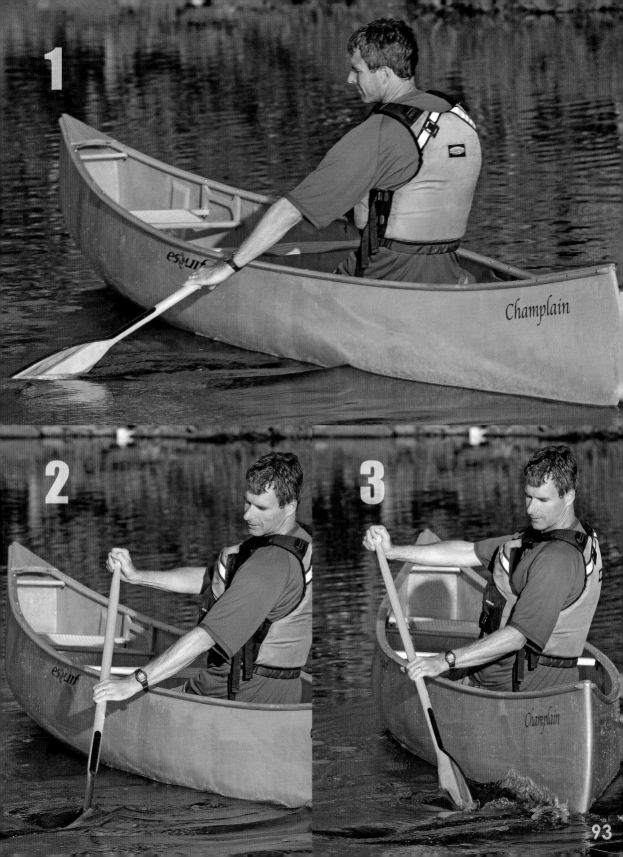

LATERAL STROKES

DRAW

The draw stroke allows you to pull the canoe towards your paddle. It can be used to move the canoe sideways in a slide slip, or to assist in spinning the canoe to face a new direction. It is one of the easiest maneuvering strokes to perform.

Begin the draw by placing the paddle vertically in the water with the power face parallel to the gunwales, at arms length, and adjacent to your knee. Twist your upper body to face your paddle so that you can, as always, use your torso muscles for power. The degree of torso twist should not exceed your comfort level because even a small amount of rotation will help the stroke. Now, pull the paddle toward the canoe in line with the position of your knee. Before the paddle hits your canoe, twist your control hand thumb away from you to rotate the blade 90 degrees in the water. You can now slice it away from the canoe to return it to the starting position of the stroke. Twist your control hand thumb back to where it was at the beginning of the stroke, so that the blade is once again parallel to the gunwales. Repeat the draw as often as necessary to slide slip or spin the canoe in the desired direction.

1

The draw stroke begins with the paddle positioned to the side of the canoe, adjacent to your knee, with arms fully extended and your torso rotated to face the paddle.

2

A vertical paddle will make your draw stroke the most efficient. To get your paddle vertical, reach across the canoe with the control hand.

3

With the blade planted deeply in the water, pull the power face towards your body.

4

Before the paddle hits the canoe, twist your control hand thumb away from you to rotate the blade 90 degrees.

5

Slice your paddle blade back out to where it started.

6

Once it's there, twist the blade back into position for another draw stroke.

PRY

The pry stroke is used to move a stationary canoe away from the paddle blade. The paddle is used as a lever to pry against the gunwale of the canoe, which forces the boat away from the planted blade. This is a very powerful stroke and can easily move a heavily loaded canoe.

Position the paddle vertically against the gunwale close to your knee with the power face against the hull. Similar to the draw stroke, you should turn your upper body to face the paddle. Stack your hands one above the other.

The pry begins with the control hand pulling towards the interior of the canoe. Pull in just far enough to position your hand above your on-side knee. Pulling too far will cause the paddle to lift water and the canoe to wobble. Once the pry is complete, twist the control hand to point the thumb away from you and slice the blade back to the hull, ready for another pry.

A number of pries can be repeated in sequence to move the canoe sideways as far as necessary.

1. Hold the paddle vertically against the gunwale adjacent to your knee with both hands stacked one over the other, above the gunwale.

2. Pry the paddle off the gunwale by pulling inward with the control hand. Do not pull it past the mid-point of the canoe.

3. To repeat the pry, rotate the blade 90 degrees by twisting your control hand thumb away from you, and then slice blade back to its starting point.

STABILITY STROKES

Falling out of a canoe happens to everyone once in a while—one moment everything is fine, then suddenly kerplunk, you're in the water. Just as annoying is when you know you are about to tip or fall over the side, and time itself slows to a crawl as if to watch the event unfold. Upsets sometimes results from waves; other times it's simply our own careless movement in the canoe that causes the problem. These scenarios have one thing in common: you lost your balance and were unable to regain control before hitting the water.

Understanding what it takes to remain balanced goes a long way in preventing capsizing or carelessly tumbling over the side of your canoe. Canoes themselves are remarkably stable crafts, so let's focus on body posture as a device to stay upright in the canoe. Good paddling posture normally has your head perched over your tailbone which is likewise centered over the keel line of the boat. Loss of balance almost always starts with the head shifting too far to the side towards a gunwale, and away from the midline of the canoe. After that, the rest is history.

Stability strokes such as the low brace and righting pry have but one goal: they are the tools used to re-position your head over your tailbone, and as a result, allow you to regain your balance and proper paddling posture. Once you've recovered your balance, your legs can again take control of the boat and allow you to move the canoe through the waves while your upper body remains steady and balanced.

1

The low brace uses the backside of your paddle blade out at 90 degrees from your boat.

2

Smacking the water with the flat backside of your paddle will provide enough momentary support for you to re-balance your body in the canoe.

LOW BRACE

The low brace is the stability stroke used to correct for loss of balance towards your on-side. If you feel your weight begin to fall towards your paddle side, and loss of balance is imminent, then smoothly assume the low brace position.

The low brace is performed by placing the paddle 90 degrees (perpendicular) to the gunwale with the back face down. This positions your knuckles on both hands facing down. Be sure to position your control hand in front of your stomach and extend your shaft hand outside the canoe over the water. In this position the paddle becomes something like an outrigger.

Once the paddle is in the low brace position, push the paddle face down so that it becomes a platform to launch yourself back into a balanced sitting position. The paddle doesn't need to be pushed very hard. The purpose of the blade is to give you just enough support to allow you to reposition your upper body, mainly your head, back into the upright paddling posture.

Your head has the greatest influence on maintaining balance, so you'll need a strategy on how to use it to regain stability. The effectiveness of the low brace can be significantly boosted by dropping your head toward the paddle shaft at the beginning of the stroke, although this will feel very counter-intuitive. Next, swing your head across the canoe from your on-side gunwale to the off-side gunwale and finish by sitting upright.

When a swing of your head and low brace are performed together, almost all unplanned on-side dips in the lake can be avoided. Lowering your head and using the paddle to support swinging your upper body across the canoe is so effective that you can often keep the canoe upright—even after a gunwale has begun to ship water. This is one amazing stroke, but the secret to its success is in using your head.

3

Dropping your head towards your paddle shaft lets your knees level the canoe.

4

Once the canoe has levelled out, assume a stable paddling posture with your head centered inside the canoe.

RIGHTING PRY

If you feel that you are losing your balance towards your off-side, use the righting pry on your on-side to maintain your stability. Although labeled a pry, this stroke is a powerful tool for keeping the canoe upright and providing the leverage to pull your body back in when you're falling overboard.

Begin the righting pry by slicing the paddling blade, edge first, straight toward the canoe so that the shaft contacts the hull in the area between your hip and knee. With the paddle vertical, twist the blade with the control hand so that the back face is against the side of the canoe. Now pull the paddle grip from its upright position, downward, across and in front of your chest, which will cause the power face to pry water away from the canoe.

This levering motion actually lifts a considerable amount of water with the blade. The resistance of the water gives you the purchase required to pull your falling body back into the canoe. Once you've pulled yourself back upright, assume a good paddling posture and you'll discover that you are back in a balanced position.

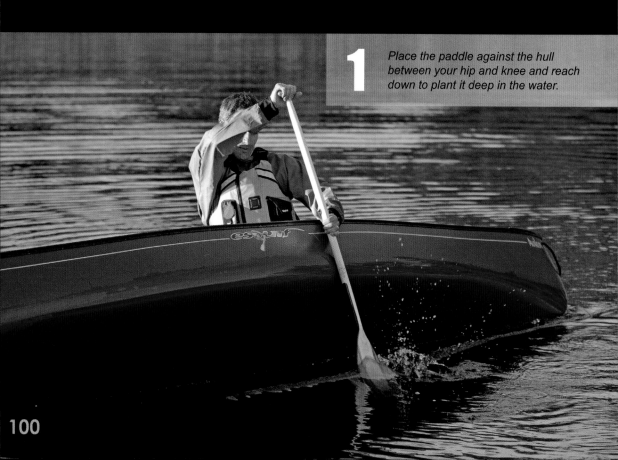

1 *Place the paddle against the hull between your hip and knee and reach down to plant it deep in the water.*

2 Once the blade is firmly planted, pull your control hand inward with your shaft hand held against the gunwale.

3 These movements pry the gunwale downward and level off the canoe.

THE ESSENTIAL MANEUVERS

STRAIGHT AHEAD

STRAIGHT BACKWARD

PIVOTS

SIDE SLIPS

MOVING TURNS

Canoe maneuvers fall into two categories: static and dynamic. Static maneuvers are performed when the canoe is starting from a standstill. Typically, these maneuvers are necessary to reposition the canoe prior to paddling somewhere. Examples of static moves include pivots and side slips. Dynamic maneuvers occur when the canoe is in motion. Examples of dynamic moves include carving turns to the right or left.

Performing static maneuvers like spins and side slips demonstrate the most basic cause and effect relationship between the paddle and the canoe. The canoe is standing still prior to your first stroke, and then it moves in response to your paddle movements. Newton's Third Law of Motion states: for every action there is an equal and opposite reaction.

Dynamic maneuvers are more complex because the water moving beneath the hull of your canoe influences how your boat behaves. Your paddle strokes therefore have to work with the way that water affects the responsiveness of the hull while it is in motion. During dynamic maneuvers, tandem partners are dependent on one another. While they may individually complete different strokes at different times throughout a maneuver, they work as a team following a specifically designed stroke sequence for a mutually determined purpose.

In this chapter, the stroke sequences used for the most common static and dynamic flat water canoeing maneuvers are mapped out in detail for tandem bow and stern, as well as for solo boats.

Successfully paddling a canoe in a straight line demands a keen awareness of where the bow is pointing and how the prevailing wind and wave conditions may affect your course. As you paddle your canoe, you'll likely find that the job of maintaining a straight course is easy in calm conditions. On windy days, the task of tracking a canoe can be much more difficult. Tracking the canoe will be much easier if you carefully watch for any veering to the side. Correcting any sideways motion early is much easier than letting it develop into an unplanned turn.

Solo paddlers and stern paddlers of tandem canoes use the same strokes to steer their boats. Bow paddlers traditionally don't participate in adjusting the course of a moving tandem canoe. Besides, it's difficult for any help offered by the bow paddler to effectively compete against the pinning waves that are always present around the bow of a canoe in motion.

The J stroke is the stroke of choice for maintaining a straight course. A skilled stern paddler learns to adjust the force of the stroke in response to the tendency of the canoe to veer away from their paddling side. Windy conditions, particularly when the wind is coming from your non-paddling side, will necessitate a much stronger J stroke than what is needed in calm conditions. If the wind is approaching your paddling side, you may find that you can skip some J strokes altogether and use simple forward strokes to maintain a straight course. In more extreme situations, if an on-side wind causes the canoe to turn toward your paddle side, adjust your forward stroke so that it becomes more like a solo forward sweep. With the forward sweep you will still propel the canoe forward but with a considerable course correction to the off-side, which will counteract the turning effect of the wind.

Depending on where you choose to launch your canoe, you may find that it's necessary to move backward away from a dock or shore. In general, other than boat positioning, backward travel is less common in flat water paddling than it is in whitewater paddling. (In rapids, reverse strokes represent the foundation for a maneuver called a "back ferry", which can help keep the canoe dry in rapids).

Moving backward represents an opportunity to use some of the fancier reverse strokes like the reverse J stroke from the tandem bow position, or the cross-back stroke in the solo canoe.

STRAIGHT BACKWARD

As with paddling forward, stroking in unison is also the most efficient way to paddle when you are going backward.

TANDEM

Moving backward in the tandem canoe presents some challenges for you and your partner because neither of you can easily see where you want to go. Patience and good communication are the keys to your success. In the tandem canoe, be prepared for the role reversal that accompanies back paddling. For reverse paddling, the bow person becomes the one responsible for steering the canoe, and the stern partner focuses on providing backward momentum.

In the bow, use the reverse J stroke for straight backward travel—the J portion of the stroke provides the prying motion necessary to keep the canoe tracking in a straight line. Turns are accomplished by the bow partner using draws or cross draws as necessary to point the stern in the desired direction. Throughout the backward travel, the stern person will provide reverse strokes timed to match the strokes of the bow paddler.

SOLO

In solo canoes, you can use a whole host of strokes to move backward and control the direction of the canoe. The reverse J stroke is typically your first choice for moving straight back with the J portion of the stroke keeping the canoe tracking in a straight line. You can alternate on-side reverse strokes with cross-back strokes to balance the natural tendency of the canoe to veer after each stroke, and this will also move the canoe straight back. Similar to the tandem bow position, solo canoeists can choose draws and cross draws to turn the canoe and point the stern wherever they need to go.

PIVOTS

Pivot maneuvers spin the canoe around its pivot point, which is located in the center of the canoe. Pivots assist in positioning the canoe so that it is pointing in the correct direction before setting off on your chosen course. Once you are pointed in the right direction, you are ready to go!

TANDEM

In tandem canoes, partners first agree on whether they will spin the canoe clockwise or counterclockwise. To pivot, partners will perform the same stroke in time with one another, with the stern partner following the lead of the bow person. Select either the draw or pry stroke to turn the canoe, depending on which direction you want to spin.

To spin in the direction of the bow person's on-side, both partners will perform the draw stroke. To spin in the other direction, each person will use pry strokes. Repeat as many strokes as necessary to turn the canoe in the direction you intend to paddle.

Tandem pivots to the bow paddler's off-side require both paddlers to use pry strokes. The bow position sets the pace for the stroke with the stern paddler following the bow paddler's lead.

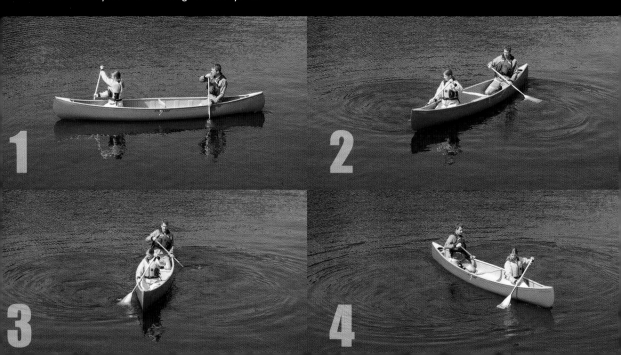

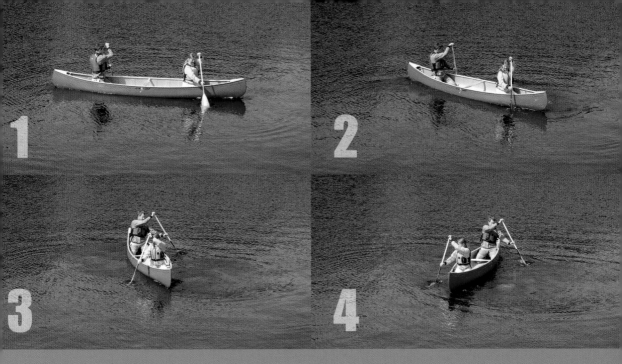

Tandem pivots to the bow person's on-side require that both paddlers use draw strokes. For a smooth spinning motion, strokes are performed in unison and with equal force.

SOLO

In the solo canoe, forward and reverse sweep strokes are used to pivot the canoe. In wider canoes, it is often to your advantage to lean the boat slightly toward your paddle to help you reach out for the sweep stroke. Solo pivots are easier if you are sitting very close to the middle of the canoe. Some canoeists, however, will prefer to sit on the bow seat facing the stern when paddling solo. In this case, a slight lean toward the middle of the canoe will assist in centering the stroke closer to the pivot point of the canoe.

Moving sideways away from a dock may be your first encounter with the side slip maneuver. Before paddling away from shore, you'll likely have to provide some additional space around the canoe for paddle strokes. Select from the draw or pry strokes to move away from your launching spot. Throughout the stroke, maintain a normal paddling posture and keep the hull of the canoe level. Whether in tandem or solo, moving sideways a little will likely be all that is needed to position the canoe for your first forward strokes.

1. *Side slips use draw and pry strokes to move the canoe sideways.*

2. *In tandem, bow and stern paddlers use opposite strokes in unison.*

3. *By using equal force, the tandem canoe will move sideways without spinning.*

SIDE SLIPS

1

TANDEM

In a tandem canoe, time your strokes so that both you and your partner stroke together, with the bow person setting the pace. In the tandem canoe, the stroke you use will be the opposite of your partner's because you are paddling on different sides of the boat. For example, a draw at one end of the canoe will be complemented by a pry at the other end, and the boat will move smoothly to the side.

SOLO

In the solo canoe, side slips will also rely on the draw or pry depending on which direction you need to travel. Stroke placement may vary as a result of where you are sitting in the canoe. Some solo canoes have you positioned close to the mid-point of the boat, while others have you closer to the stern. If you want the side slip to move you straight to the side, you'll have to make sure that your strokes are placed as close to the center of the canoe as possible. Regardless of where you are sitting, try to place the stroke near the middle of the canoe. If you are sitting closer to the stern, you will have to reach a little further.

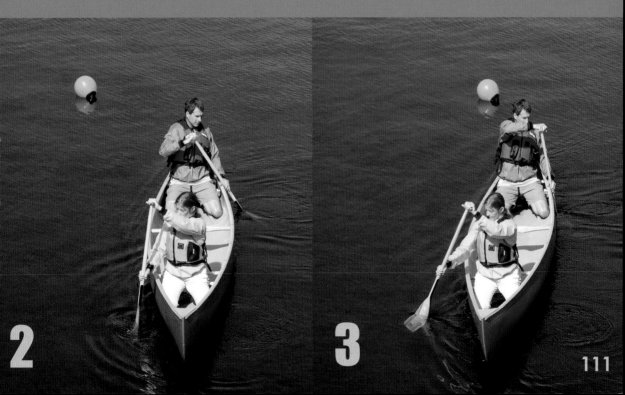

2

3

MOVING TURNS

To turn the canoe once it is in motion, you must take into account that the water, moving beneath the canoe, affects the way the boat responds to strokes. It requires that you complete turning strokes in a special order. For example, the first turning stroke of a maneuver initiates the turn. The sequence continues with additional strokes that are selected to provide boat control until the turn is completed.

This sequence of strokes used to turn the canoe, regardless of whether you are in a tandem or solo, includes four parts. Because all dynamic maneuvers require momentum, forward strokes are at the start of all turning sequences to provide the necessary propulsion to keep the canoe in motion. The actual turn begins with a stern initiation stroke that sets the canoe onto an arcing path. Following this is a bow control stroke to fine-tune the arc. Finally, all maneuvers are completed with more forward strokes to re-establish your forward momentum.

The most vital stroke in the four stroke sequence is the stern initiation. Choose from either the stern draw or stern pry to begin turning the canoe left or right. Recall that as a byproduct of the canoe moving forward, the bow waves essentially lock the canoe into traveling in the direction that the bow is pointing. To unlock the bow, you slide the stern to the left or right, which unbalances the bow waves and points the bow in the direction you've chosen.

The next stroke in sequence is the bow control stroke. Choose from either the bow draw or cross-bow draw. These strokes act as bow rudders to control how tightly the canoe turns. The bow draw and cross draw only work once the bow has been freed of the pinning waves by the preceding stern initiation stroke.

Momentum is maintained throughout the maneuver because there is always at least one person paddling forward at any given point in the turn. Because the canoe is in motion during the turn, keeping your balance is integral. Tilting the canoe in the same direction of the turn will keep both you and your partner stable and counter the tendency of the canoe, or perhaps your body, to tip toward the outside of the turn. It's very much like leaning a bicycle to keep your balance as you ride around a bend.

In the tandem canoe, tilting and performing the four stroke sequence will be enhanced by good communication between partners. Talk to your partner and use clear, easily understood language. It can be difficult to hear above the background sounds of rustling leaves or waves lapping against the canoe. Speak deliberately with as few words as possible. For example directions can be simply stated left, or right as necessary. From the stern, let your partner know when you have initiated a turn so they can follow with a bow control stroke. For successful and graceful turns, always follow the four stroke sequence.

Once a moving turn has been initiated, the bow paddler focuses on controlling the turn while the stern person maintains momentum.

Tilting the canoe on edge helps the canoe carve a turn and maintain stability.

EDGING THE CANOE

Edging refers to paddling the canoe while it is tilted onto its chine (the chine is the edge between side wall and the canoe bottom.) The two common reasons to edge the canoe are to maintain stability during turns, and to allow the hull to carve a better arc when going around a bend. To achieve the benefits of edging, you'll want to choose the chine that is on the inside of the turn. This is called the inside edge.

A characteristic of almost any boat is the tendency for it to slide to the outside of the curve when it is paddled through a turn. This slide is always more evident in the stern because the bow of the boat is sandwiched between bow waves that help to keep the front of the canoe on track. Tilting or edging is necessary because without it,

the sliding stern will catch its outside edge on the water passing beneath the chine. In many cases, catching an edge will upset your balance and cause a severe wobble, or worse, a capsized canoe.

Edging also makes turning in an arcing path easier because it changes what part of the hull is in contact with the water, and the different shape of the hull on edge improves its ability to carve. When on edge, the canoe's "footprint" is shortened and narrowed. Think of this change as creating a cutting blade with the chine of the canoe. As the canoe enters into a turn, edge the canoe and use the chine to cut a curving path in the direction you intend to paddle. Edging reduces skidding and improves your stability.

TANDEM ON-SIDE TURNS

The tandem on-side turn uses the following four stroke sequence to turn the canoe to the bow person's on-side.

1. **Bow:** Forward stroke.
   Stern: Forward stroke.
   Both paddlers tilt the canoe toward the inside of the turn.

2. **Bow:** Forward stroke.
   Stern: Stern draw to initiate the turn.
   Both paddlers continue to tilt the canoe toward the inside of the turn.

3. **Bow:** Bow draw to control the sharpness of the turn.
   Stern: Forward stroke.
   Both paddlers continue to tilt the canoe toward the inside of the turn.

4. **Bow:** Forward stroke.
   Stern: Forward stroke with stern pry to stop turn.
   Both paddlers level the canoe.

Working as a team, tandem paddlers use the stern position to initiate the turn, and bow position to control the turn. Both paddlers provide momentum when not actively involved with a steering stroke.

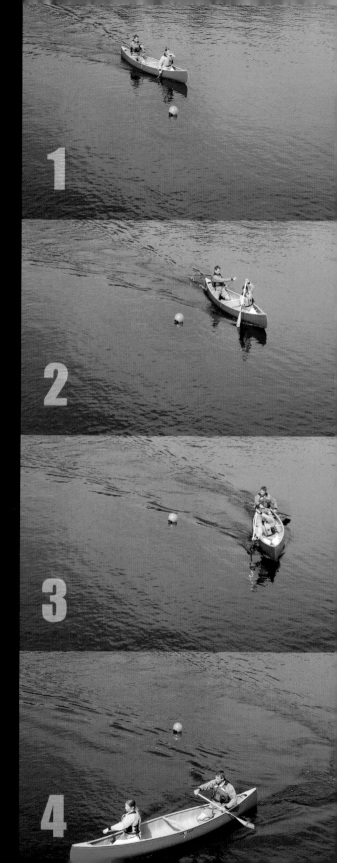

TANDEM OFF-SIDE TURNS

The tandem off-side turn also uses the four stroke sequence, and will turn the canoe to the bow person's off-side.

1. **Bow:**   Forward stroke.
   Stern: Forward stroke.
   Both paddlers tilt the canoe toward the inside of the turn.

2. **Bow:**   Forward stroke.
   Stern: Stern pry to initiate the turn.
   Both paddlers continue to tilt the canoe toward the inside of the turn.

3. **Bow:**   Cross bow draw to control the sharpness of the turn.
   Stern: Forward stroke.
   Both paddlers continue to tilt the canoe toward the inside of the turn.

4. **Bow:**   Forward stroke.
   Stern: Forward stroke.
   Both paddlers level the canoe.

Throughout moving turns, there is usually at least one paddler using forward strokes to maintain the forward momentum. Forward momentum combined with tilt help the canoe carve a smooth and efficient turn.

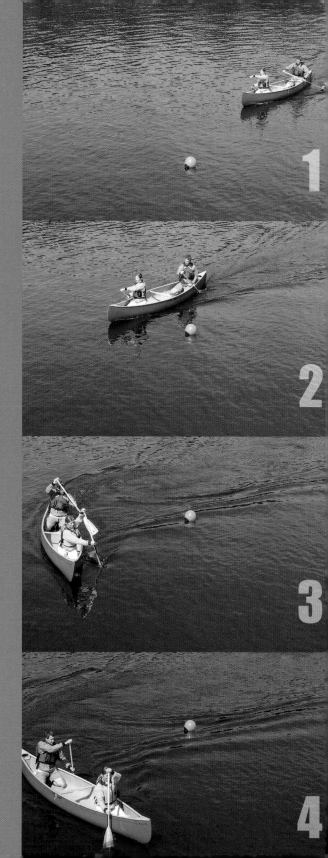

SOLO ON-SIDE TURNS

The solo on-side turn also uses the four stroke sequence, and turns the canoe to the solo paddler's on-side.

1. Forward stroke.
   Tilt the canoe toward the inside of the turn.

2. Stern pry to initiate the turn.
   Continue to tilt the canoe toward the inside of the turn.

3. Bow draw to control the sharpness of the turn.
   Continue to tilt the canoe toward the inside of the turn.

4. Forward stroke with stern draw to stop the turn
   and straighten the course of the canoe.
   Level the canoe.

Paddling solo with the boat heeled increases your maneuverability and makes it easier to turn the canoe.

1

2

3

4

It is important that a solo moving turn is initiated with plenty of forward speed. Enough glide is needed to carve an efficient turn while the forward stroke is temporarily abandoned so that a control stroke from the bow can be executed.

SOLO OFF-SIDE TURNS

The solo off-side turn is also completed with the four stroke sequence, and turns the canoe to the solo paddler's off-side.

1. Forward stroke.
   Tilt the canoe toward the inside of the turn.

2. Stern draw to initiate the turn.
   Continue to tilt the canoe toward the inside of the turn.

3. Cross bow draw to control the sharpness of the turn.
   Continue to tilt the canoe toward the inside of the turn.

4. Cross forward stroke stops the turn and provices forward momentum.
   Level the canoe.

5. Forward stroke.
   Maintain a level canoe.

The solo off-side moving turn uses the cross bow draw to control the turn while the canoe carves on edge. By turning the cross bow draw into a cross forward stroke at the end of the turn, the paddler can both straighten the canoe's course and accelerate out of the turn.

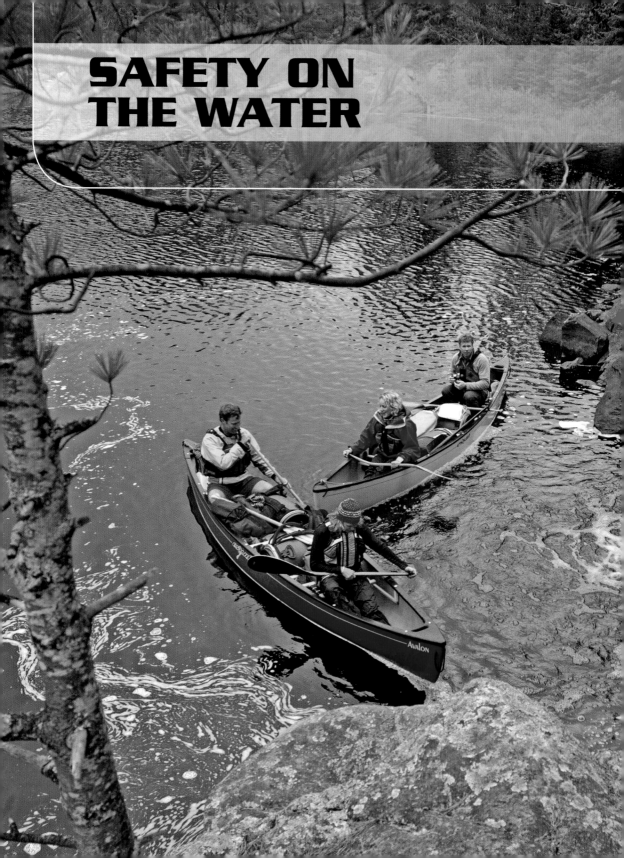

SAFETY ON
THE WATER

6

WEATHER

LAKE HAZARDS

RIVER HAZARDS

CAPSIZE RECOVERIES

You'll be happy to hear that canoeing is a remarkably safe and user-friendly activity. In fact, compared to most other outdoor activities, the chances of getting hurt while canoeing are very small. However, if things do go wrong when canoeing, the fact that you're on the water means that situations can become very serious, very quickly. For this reason it is important that you understand and appreciate the risks and hazards involved with canoeing, and that you assume a conservative and safety-conscious attitude when making decisions on the water.

Avoiding dangerous situations on the water is surprisingly easy. First and foremost, understand that alcohol and boating simply don't go together. Regrettably, alcohol is a major factor in too many boating accidents. It's also critical that you wear a PFD whenever you're on the water. By investing in a PFD that is designed to be as comfortable and as unrestricting as possible, you'll eliminate virtually any reason for wanting to remove it. On a similar note, you need to dress for the conditions. Cold water represents the biggest hazard, as cold water immersion can result in hypothermia very quickly. If you're paddling in cold water, you need to be more conservative with all your decisions. Paddle only in calm conditions, stay close to shore, never paddle alone, and keep in mind that you're better off overdressing and being too warm than being too cold.

One of the easiest ways to stay safe and ensure that your paddling experience is fun for everyone is to choose an appropriate paddling location. One of the greatest things about canoeing is that there are so many great spots to explore, whether you live near a lake, river, or pond. Most importantly, you'll want to pick a location that is sheltered from both wind and waves. The ideal paddling environment has a good access point for launching, an unobstructed shoreline for easy landings, and minimal motorized on-water traffic. Seek out calm bays or quiet lakes and river ways. Although it can be tempting to search out the most remote location possible, bear in mind that if you ever did need a little assistance, it's nice to know that there will be someone around who can lend a hand. By the same token, that's why it's not a great idea to paddle alone. There really is safety in numbers when it comes to being out on the water, so always paddle with a group, or at least another buddy who can come to your aid (or vice versa) should an unforeseen situation arise.

WEATHER

Weather should play a significant role in your decision to go paddling. Local forecasts should be reviewed prior to paddling to assess wind, temperature, chance of precipitation or risk of severe weather. Always err on the side of caution and avoid weather conditions in which you feel uncomfortable.

In large bodies of water, your biggest weather concerns will be wind and waves. Strong winds can push you around and make it impossible to move forward. Gusts of wind can even catch you off-guard and flip you over. Furthermore, wind can drum up waves surprisingly quickly, which can complicate a safe egress to shore. It's actually pretty easy to avoid getting caught out in nasty, windy and wavy conditions—avoid open water and stay in calm, protected areas.

Rain on its own is no big deal when you're out in a canoe. In fact, paddling in the rain can be a very relaxing experience. Unfortunately, rain can be accompanied by other forms of weather. Dealing with wind may be your first consideration, but what about thunder and lightning? If you hear thunder, you know that there's lightning around, and lightning is very dangerous to anyone out on the water. When you're on the water, you're usually the highest point for quite a distance in any direction, making you a perfect lightning rod. At the first hint of thunder or lightning, get off the water immediately and wait until the storm passes by. Although it's rare, people have also been struck by lightning by heading out too soon after they think the storm has passed—there can be a lot of electricity in the trailing edge of a storm system. A good rule of thumb is to wait 15 minutes after the last flash of lightning before you get back on the water.

Storms can travel with surprising speed, so always keep an eye on the sky.

LAKE HAZARDS

Many lakes represent true multi-use recreational areas. Power boats, sail boats, jet skis, kayaks and canoes all use some lakes simultaneously. Beware of fast-moving water craft, and if they are present, stay close to shore because most power boats are more likely to travel out in open water. If you are crossing a lake and find that you are being approached by a power boat, assume that they can not see you and make an evasive maneuver. Wave your paddle for extra visibility if they come too close and you think a collision is possible. Often, canoes are difficult to see from a motor boat because they float so much lower in the water.

Some lakes are well known for producing large waves in windy conditions. Be alert for changing weather conditions that may necessitate moving off the water, or at least to the protection of bays or islands. If you canoe in an area that has been recently logged, beware of partially submerged logs or "dead heads" because these can upset even the most stable canoes if you collide with one.

Large lakes can present some of the most challenging paddling conditions—heavy winds and large waves. Unless you're confident with your ability to recover from a capsize in open water, you should always stay within swimming distance from the shore.

RIVER HAZARDS

Moving water, even slow-moving water, is a powerful force. It's important that you are aware of the hazards that are associated with any rivers and streams that may have current present. Even calm rivers may have short sections of current, even rapids, which interrupt long sections of flat water. Unless you are aware of the hazards and are knowledgeable about how to mitigate the risks, avoid currents and rapids.

STRAINERS

Strainers are probably the most common and dangerous obstacle on any river. A strainer is a pile of logs or other debris that has been stacked up by the current over time, usually against a rock or bridge abutments. They are called strainers because they work just like pouring pasta and hot water into a colander. The pasta is stopped by the colander while the water passes through the holes. With a strainer on the river, a canoe can get pinned like the noodles against the strainer while the water passes through. The difference is that the water never stops flowing on the river and the longer you and your boat are pinned there, the worse it gets. It can be extremely dangerous to get caught against a strainer—even in what you think is fairly light current—and if you get pulled under, rescue can be very difficult. If your canoe gets pinned and you can still get yourself out and on to land, it is often wise to consider abandoning your boat and get help later to pull it out. A boat and gear can be replaced—you can't be. Of course, the best thing to do with strainers is to identify them from upstream and give them a wide berth, completely avoiding them from the start.

LOW HEAD DAMS

Low head dams are an extremely hazardous obstacle on the river. For starters, they are very difficult to see from upstream until it is too late

with a perfectly horizontal pour-over line, causing it to form a perfect recirculating hydraulic on the other side. Among fire departments and river rescue circles, low head dams are referred to as "drowning machines". The only plan of attack in this situation is to know whether the river you are paddling has one on it or not. If it does, know where it is, take out well above it, and portage to a spot well below it before putting back in. Leave nothing to chance with a low head dam. Have an avoidance plan and stick to it.

FOOT ENTRAPMENT

The foot entrapment is one of the most common causes of death in shallow, moving water. What happens is that when standing up in current, your foot can get lodged between rocks or anything else on the riverbed. With your foot stuck, the current can easily knock you over and even a light current can make it impossible to get up or unstuck. Foot entrapments can easily lead to a drowning in as little as two feet of water. Being a good swimmer is irrelevant. Avoiding a foot entrapment is easy—simply don't wade out into fast-moving water. If for some reason you do find yourself swimming in fast-moving current, resist the temptation to stand up and walk to shore even if you're in only a few feet of water. Swim your way right into shore and out of the main current before you attempt to stand.

CAPSIZE RECOVERIES

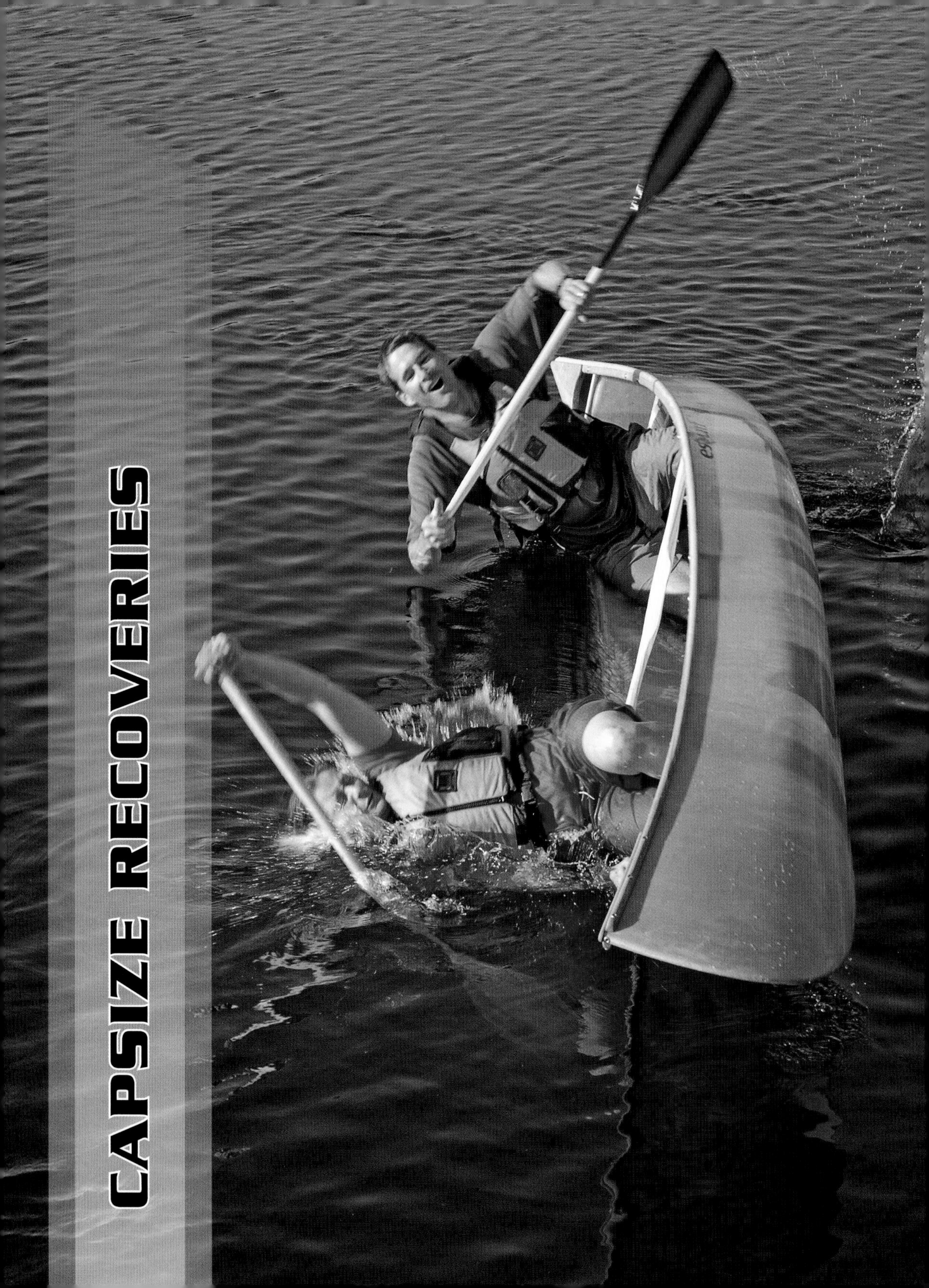

Enjoyment of any outdoor adventure is enhanced by good preparation. Flat water canoeing is no exception. Practicing your paddling skills, being well-equipped, and having a plan in the event of a capsized canoe are all necessary before a day on the water. Although canoe capsizes are fairly rare in flat water, the risk of cold water immersion or an extended swim to shore in a situation where help is unlikely, make rescue skills necessary. This segment will be about preparing for both assisted and self-rescue techniques.

Canoe capsizes can occur unexpectedly. Even when conditions seem ideal, the unthinkable can happen—your boat flips over. More common are canoe swims associated with high wind or waves. Be aware of changing conditions and head for shore when a situation threatens your comfort level. Wearing your PFD is always advisable when venturing out in a canoe.

If you fall out of your canoe, or if you lose your balance and it flips over, conventional wisdom encourages you to stay with your canoe. Depending on the circumstances, however, staying with your canoe may be either a good or a bad idea. Your decision to stay with your boat, or to leave it and swim for shore, will be based on a number of factors. Plan your decision ahead of time so you're prepared to act quickly if your canoe capsizes.

Staying with the canoe may be your best plan in some of the following conditions:

- Assistance is close at hand, and you will be removed from the water quickly.
- You can perform a self-rescue in a timely manner.
- Swimming to shore is risky because of distance or swimming ability.
- Cold water immersion and the risk of hypothermia is not an immediate threat.

Staying with your canoe offers the advantage of providing flotation and it also increases your visibility to rescuers. On overnight or longer canoe trips, it is to your advantage to be recovered with your gear because you'll rely on the equipment in your canoe for food and shelter.

Abandoning your canoe is considered a more drastic response to an over-turned boat. Consider leaving your canoe in the following conditions:

- Cold water immersion and hypothermia is an imminent threat.
- Self-rescue in a timely manner is unlikely.
- Assisted rescue is unlikely to occur.
- Off-shore wind or out-going tide will carry you further away from shore.
- The risk of swimming, in your judgment, is less of a risk than staying with the canoe.

Swimming for shore may provide the advantage of getting out of cold water sooner and reducing the potential of hypothermia. Once on shore, assistance and/or communication may be available if you are paddling in a populated area.

Capsizing your canoe may not be a common occurrence, but if you plan on paddling in anything but the most sheltered conditions and/or further from shore than you can easily swim, practicing how to get back into an overturned boat becomes as essential as learning to paddle.

Flat water canoeing is often enjoyed in small groups with friends who, like yourself, also appreciate the outdoors as experienced from a watery vantage point. Of course paddling in groups offers a safety advantage because assistance, in the event of a boat overturning, is close at hand. The canoe-over-canoe rescue can be performed by fellow boaters paddling either canoe or kayak. With the assistance offered by a second boat, the capsized canoe can be turned upright and emptied, and the swimming paddlers can be helped back into their boat. With practice, this rescue technique takes only a few minutes.

Begin a canoe-over-canoe rescue by first confirming that the swimming paddlers are safe and accounted for. Next, position the rescue boat perpendicular to the overturned boat and have the swimmers grasp the ends of the rescue boat. Having the swimmers holding the bow and stern of your canoe adds stability while keeping them in a safe location throughout the rescue. Have the swimmers store their paddles in the rescue canoe for safekeeping.

The overturned canoe is grasped near its end, lifted, then pulled across your gunwales. Sometimes, tipping the overturned canoe slightly to one side while lifting it helps to break the suction created by the airlock that often occurs under a capsized canoe. Pull the canoe over your gunwales until it is balanced evenly end to end. Once emptied, the canoe can be flipped upright, slipped back into the water, and held parallel to your canoe.

By firmly holding the gunwales of the two canoes together, the rescued canoe can be stabilized to allow the re-entry of the swimming paddlers. It is easiest if the paddlers attempt to climb in mid-ship where the gunwale is closer to the water and the canoe is more stable. As the swimmer attempts to climb into the canoe, allow the far gunwale to drop to water level to reduce the climbing height necessary to get back into the boat. As a swimmer, keep your body (and center of gravity) low as you wiggle back into your canoe.

Continue holding the canoes together until the rescued paddlers have re-established a stable kneeling position in the canoe and have their paddles at the ready for their first strokes.

1. Having made sure the swimmer is safe at your bow, position your canoe perpendicular to the capsized boat.

2. Grab the bow and the closest gunwale, and then lift the boat up and pull it across your canoe.

3. Once the boat is out of the water, roll the canoe upright, away from you.

4. Slide the canoe back into the water and hold it steady beside your canoe.

5. Approaching from mid-ship, the swimmer uses a strong kick and push up to climb into the canoe.

6. The swimmer stays as low as possible in the canoe until they are back in their sitting position.

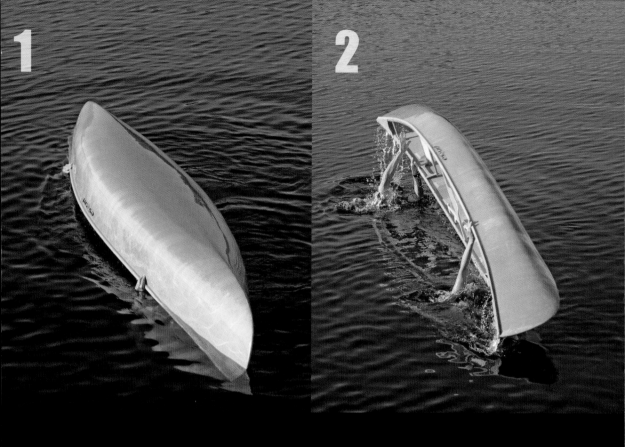

CAPISTRANO FLIP

The Capistrano Flip is a self-rescue technique that can be used by tandem or solo canoeists who have capsized in deep water. The maneuver is moderately difficult as it requires that you lift the canoe completely out of the water! This job is made easier by paddling a light weight canoe.

To do a Capistrano Flip, position yourself and your partner beneath the overturned canoe at opposite ends of the craft. Face one another so that you can easily communicate and time your movements. From your position under the canoe, lift one gunwale to scoop as much air beneath the overturned hull as possible. Next, lift one gunwale slightly above the water to break the airlock. Together, do a strong scissors kick upward and heave one gunwale in an upward arc to flip the canoe upright. Support the other gunwale

just above the water to minimize shipping water into what should now be your upright canoe.

With the canoe upright, both paddlers can re-enter from opposite sides of the canoe. Again in a coordinated effort, both paddlers begin by holding opposing gunwales close to mid-ship—one on the bow side of the center yoke, and the other on the stern side. With vigorous kicking, both paddlers hoist themselves back into the canoe simultaneously to keep the canoe balanced.

Even if the Capistrano Flip was only partially effective in draining the boat, the result should be that both paddlers are once again back in the safety of the canoe. Together you can either bail the remaining water, or paddle to shore and empty in the relative security of shallow water.

1. Paddlers set-up beneath the canoe by grasping the gunwales near their respective seats.

2. In unison, use strong scissors kicks and fling one edge of the canoe up and over your heads.

3. Hold on to the other gunwale to prevent the wind blowing the upright canoe away.

4. Re-enter in unison from opposite sides of the canoe.

5. Keep your bodies as low as possible to keep the canoe stable.

6. Through every step, communicate with your partner and work as a team.

To perform a shake-out, rock the boat back and forth so that the water trapped inside splashes over the gunwales and out of the canoe.

Once most of the water is out, you can re-enter from mid-ship and then bail the remaining water out.

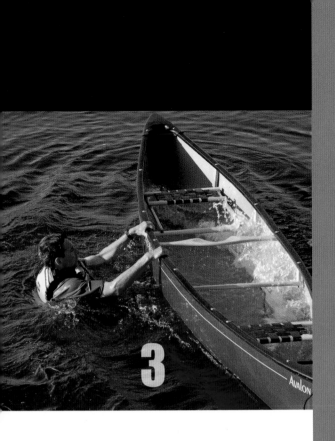

Another self-rescue technique is the shake-out. Effective with solo or tandem canoes, the shake-out is best performed by just one paddler because coordinating the movement with a partner is difficult. After the canoe has capsized, turn the canoe over so that it is in the upright position. Grip the canoe at one end and push it forcefully downward and forward. This sloshes the water out of the canoe. After repeated thrusts the water is progressively emptied from the boat. This method of draining the canoe may not be as effective as the Capistrano Flip; however, it is somewhat easier to perform. Even if the canoe is only partially emptied, it can be re-entered and bailed, or simply paddled to shore and emptied.

An alternative to doing the shake-out from one end of the boat is to complete a similar self-rescue from the side of the canoe at mid-ship. Hold the gunwale near to the center thwart and push down and away from yourself. Thrust down and away repeatedly until you're satisfied that you have shaken as much water out of the canoe as possible. Once again climb in and bail the remaining water, or paddle to shore to finish the job there.

EMPTYING AT SHORE

Most deep water self-rescues will still need a trip to shore to completely empty the water out of the canoe. Although this skill is comparatively easy, there is a knack to emptying your canoe at shore. Working with your paddling partner, begin with the canoe floating upside-down in shallow water. With each partner positioned at either end of the canoe, pick up the canoe at the same time by grabbing under the deck plates. Lift the canoe up using the strength of your legs to protect your back, then turn it upright and place it back on the water.

GLOSSARY

Back face the side of the paddle blade that does not pull water during a forward canoe stroke; if the paddle blade is curved, the back face is the convex side; see also: "power face"

Bow the front end of the canoe; see also: "stern"

Canoe a watercraft propelled by a single-bladed paddle

Canoe-over-canoe a capsize recovery technique for deep water, in which the capsized canoe is emptied of water by lifting it upside-down over the gunwales of the rescue canoe

Capistrano Flip a capsize recovery technique which involves emptying the canoe by lifting it over your head while treading water, then flipping it upright

Capsize when a canoe overturns while in the water

Carve an arcing path that is achieved when the canoe is held on edge while it is moving forward; see also: "edging"

Chine the part of the hull of a canoe between the sidewall and the bottom of the canoe, usually curved

Control hand the top hand that holds the paddle's hand grip; see also: "shaft hand"

Dry bag a waterproof bag used for storage, usually having a roll-top closing system

Edging the act of tilting your canoe to one side without capsizing it, typically accomplished while still sitting in the center of the boat; see also: "heeling"

Eddy the quiet water downstream of an obstacle in current; eddies sometimes have a weaker current running in an opposite direction to the main current

Gunwale pronounced "gunnel", the structural trim running the length of the top edge of the canoe

Heeling tilting the canoe to one side by sitting off-center, a solo paddling technique; see also: "edging"

Hull the bottom of the canoe

Hypothermia a dangerous physical condition resulting from a decrease in body temperature after exposure to a cold environment, it should be identified and treated as soon as possible

Kayak a watercraft propelled by a double-bladed paddle

Keel the center ridge that runs down the length of the bottom of a canoe from bow to stern

Kevlar a strong and lightweight synthetic fiber used to make canoe hulls

Low brace a stability stroke that uses the back face of the paddle

Off-side in a solo canoe, off-side is the opposite side from which you usually hold your paddle; in a tandem canoe, off-side is the opposite side from which the bow paddler usually holds his or her paddle

On-side in a solo canoe, on-side is the side on which you usually hold your paddle; in a tandem canoe, on-side is the side on which the bow paddler usually holds his or her paddle

Paddle comprised of a shaft, a blade, and a grip, canoe paddles have a single blade for propelling a canoe through water; often the paddle grip, blade and shaft are carved from one piece of wood; kayak paddles have a shaft and two blades

Paddle grip on a canoe paddle, the handle at one end of the paddle shaft, used to hold and control the paddle

Paddle shaft the narrow bar between the paddle blade and the paddle grip

PFD Personal Floatation Device or life jacket

Pivots canoe turns that move the canoe around its center axis

Portage noun: a trail that links two navigable waterways; verb: the act of carrying a canoe and gear between navigable waterways

Port when sitting in a canoe facing the bow, port is the left side of the boat; see also: "starboard"

Power face the side of the paddle blade that pulls water during a forward canoe stroke; if the paddle blade is curved, the back face is the concave side; see also: "back face"

Righting pry a stabilizing stroke used to prevent capsizing on your off-side

Rocker the curvature of the hull from bow to stern

Roof rack a system of two bars that mount to the roof of a vehicle used for transporting canoes and other loads

Royalex® a very strong, ABS-based plastic laminate used for building canoe hulls

Self-rescue a capsize recovery technique where the capsized paddler re-enters the canoe without aid from a second party

Shaft hand the bottom hand that grips the shaft of the paddle; see also "control hand"

Shake-out a capsize recovery technique used to empty water from a capsized canoe by rocking the boat back and forth vigorously

Side slip to move the canoe sideways

Solo one paddler in a canoe; or a canoe designed to be paddled by one person

Starboard when sitting in a canoe facing the bow, starboard is the right side of the boat; see also: "port"

Stern the rear end of the canoe; see also: "bow"

Tandem two paddlers in a canoe; or a canoe designed to be paddled by two people

Thwart a cross bar between port and starboard gunwales that provides some structural integrity to the canoe

Tracking paddling a straight line

Trim refers to the relative heights of the bow and stern of a floating canoe

Tumblehome when canoe hull narrows above the waterline as it gets closer to the gunwales

Whitewater a current or moving water, in a river

Yoke a sculpted thwart at about mid-ship that is designed to rest on a person's shoulders when the canoe is upside-down and being carried solo

INDEX

More Great Books from the Heliconia Press and Fox Chapel Publishing

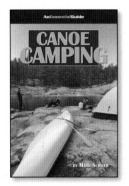

Canoe Camping
An Essential Guide
By Mark Scriver

This comprehensive guide by senior guide and World Champion paddler Mark Scriver makes canoe camping fun and safe for both new and experienced canoe trippers.

$16.95 · 112 Pages

Outdoor Parents, Outdoor Kids
The Ultimate Guide
By Eugene Buchanan

Award-winning author Eugene Buchanan extends parents a helping hand in getting their kids outside and instilling in them a respect for their health and the environment.

$19.95 · 304 Pages

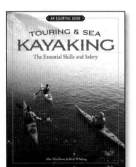

Touring & Sea Kayaking
An Essential Guide
By Alex Matthews and Ken Whiting

This guide provides beginner and experienced kayakers with the knowledge and skills necessary to safely and comfortably enjoy sea kayaking.

$19.95 · 120 Pages

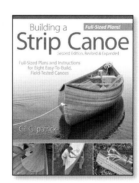

Building a Strip Canoe, Second Edition, Revised & Expanded
Full-Sized Plans and Instructions for Eight Easy-To-Build, Field-Tested Canoes
By Gil Gilpatrick

Paddle along with an expert outdoorsman and canoe builder as he shares his experience in guiding both novice and accomplished woodworkers in building a canoe with easy step-by-step instructions.

$24.95 · 112 Pages